DAILY PEACE FOR
TURBULENT TIMES

CENTERING PRAYERS

VOLUME 2

PETER TRABEN HAAS

PARACLETE PRESS
BREWSTER, MASSACHUSETTS

2024 First Printing

Centering Prayers, Volume 2: Daily Peace for Turbulent Times

ISBN 978-1-64060-921-1

Scripture quotations are from New Revised Standard Version Bible: Anglicized Edition, copyright © 1989, 1995 National Council of the Churches of Christ in the United States of America. Used by permission. All rights reserved worldwide.

The Paraclete Press name and logo (dove on cross) are trademarks of Paraclete Press.

Cover design by Paraclete Design

The Library of Congress has catalogued Volume 1 of *Centering Prayers* as follows:
Haas, Peter Traben.
Centering prayers : a one-year daily companion for going deeper into the love of God / Peter Traben Haas.
pages cm
Includes bibliographical references.
ISBN 978-1-61261-415-1 (trade pb)
1. Prayers. I. Title.
BV245.H215 2013
242'.8—dc23 2013024326

10 9 8 7 6 5 4 3 2 1

Published by Paraclete Press
Brewster, Massachusetts
www.paracletepress.com

Printed in India

I DEDICATE THESE PRAYERS TO
MY MOTHER, JENNY—

Who even without knowing it,
first formed me in the spirit of prayer,
as she lives her life looking unto the hills
from whence her strength arises.

CONTENTS

vi

PREFACE

L ike in ages past, we live in a world community of agitating divisions and intensifying fears. And like in ages past, it is a world community that desperately needs individuals and communities to be centered in Christ; to abide with Christ; to radiate Christ's healing love and joy. Yet, unlike in ages past, the scale and scope of our human imprint upon earth and eight billion conundrums of being here together, interconnected as close as a text, call, connection, click, swipe, or upload—is unprecedented, and calls forth from each of us the utmost patience, wisdom, courage, and care.

I'm writing this preface from the glorious Wright Library at Princeton Theological Seminary. It is a temple of light and learning, helping form ministers in the patterns of devotion and, ideally, providing glimpses through books into the ever-unfolding realms of theology. I've returned here to my *alma mater* for a brief discernment retreat, to slow down, to listen, to walk in the nearby forest and wait upon the Lord.

As I write this, I'm overlooking the early autumn oaks and sycamores that are just beginning to turn. It is a cool, gray day, lightly raining, and everything feels extra quiet. After four months of enduring Texas summer heat, I find this place a refuge not only for my inner being but also for my body.

Since graduating from here nearly thirty years ago, I've been humbled by life into the awareness that while there may be many ways to knowing God, there are also many ways that lead nowhere. And for the rest of my life, God willing, I aim to keep things simple and clear, and to focus on the gospel of Jesus Christ as presented and revealed in the canonical Scriptures of the Hebrew and Christian Bible.

Considering that, holding this sheaf of prayers in my hands—a weight of words formed in the early morning hours, soaked in silence, over several years—I ponder whether, perhaps, rather than *Centering Prayers*, this book of prayers could also be called *Radiating Prayers*. By radiating, I mean to convey a movement of love outward from the center toward the world, toward other hearts, toward other beings.

I say this in part because I wish to ensure that by the word *centering* we don't mean a collapsing in or a retreat from, or a quietist denial of the world and its life and people in need of care and words of nourishment, and deeds of mercy. It seems to me that the Spirit's invitation is to hold two truths equally yoked, as awkward as that can be sometimes: contemplation *and* action. Silence *and* speaking. Stillness *and* effort. Grace *and* practice. Center *and* circumference. Devotion *and* service.

It is my wish that the book of prayers you now hold in your hands or read on a screen is in service to the grace of the center meeting you just as you are, yet also calling you deeper. I believe that the center is the ever preexistent and ever eternal Word of God, who lives to nourish and encourage you to share your gifts.

As you do, you will join the confluence of others also radiating their love and devotion outward into a world community much in need of the grace that flows through the nexus of your center's union with Christ the center—a confluence that Jesus termed *abiding*. Thus, we can begin to see the lovely and resilient contours of the Christian journey: *Centering. Abiding. Radiating.*

This volume is designed as a companion resource to my book *Centering Prayers: A One-Year Daily Companion for Going Deeper into the Love of God*. In addition to personal devotion, perhaps the structuring of the book will support using these prayers for family devotions or in community worship, especially as the church moves through the various liturgical seasons of the year.

And though the prayers are intentionally brief and almost always are written in the voice of first-person singular, I invite you to adapt them to your situation and journey. Feel free to shorten or expand them, or even to shift the "I" to "We"; the "my" to "our." Read the prayer and make it your own.

Overall, this new volume of prayers continues in the same aim and vein as *Centering Prayers*, Volume 1, though with a keener attention to themes of earth, water, and sky. I pray these prayers bless you and speak to you and give voice to your own heart's articulations. Whether you read these prayers prior to your own meditative prayer or following your time in the silence, or as prayers-on-the-go, may they nourish you on your journey ever deeper into God's love, in this age and the ages to come.

We are listening and speaking together in the silence, through Jesus the Living Word, and Prince of Peace.

Peter Traben Haas

A CAUTION ON METHODS AND THE EXPERIENCE OF EMPTINESS

I'd like to share something that I have learned on my spiritual journey into and through meditative prayer methods and leading spiritual retreats: no practice of prayer, no spiritual discipline, nor path of spiritual practice, is greater than its source. The method serves, and never reigns. Prayer serves the center. And, as our life unfolds, we are held in love by the center.

Methods of prayer, modes of prayer, all manner of praying—these sacred, profound, beloved friends—are just humble servants. They are some of the many gracious and gentle ways that the Spirit of the living Jesus Christ can become available to us.

This also means that at the heart of all prayer, especially meditative, silent prayer, there isn't just passive emptiness. At the heart of prayer there is a space waiting to be filled with relationship.

Yes, sometimes, in some seasons of our spiritual journey, our prayer life may *feel as if* there is a fruitless, dark emptiness, but the emptiness is more of a fortuitous opening, like a deep passageway in a cave, opening into new territory, through which a deeper and fuller exploration of relationship with God and self and others can occur.

Perhaps it is a season of life that feels empty because we are invited to let go of some or all of the comforting fullness of our self and its stories and attachments; the no longer useful ways of being we've been carrying with us in our hearts and bodies along the way.

Through this opening, this releasing, this unencumbering of self, this letting go, a space for new possibilities emerges. An emptiness to receive more of what the Spirit is newly making available. In the silence and through the Word of God in Scripture, such as in *lectio divina*, a deeper relating becomes available to us. Preeminently, a relating with the one named before all eternity: Jesus the Christ, revealed to us by the presence and action of the Spirit through Mary.

Not knowing how it all works, we proceed in faith trusting that the language and logic of the Spirit will attune us in the silence of the center to the living Jesus Christ. And from this silence of the center, behold, words birth forth! And we hold onto these words for our life. And they hold onto us.

Following the way of Jesus Christ, we are assured that this relational center isn't just an empty silence. The silence of the center serves as an initial vestibule to relationship with God through Christ, and as a deepening union with God in the Way of Jesus. Thus, paradoxically, the silence of the center births:

Words and wisdom for us to live by.

Words to understand mysteries.

Words to listen to in seasons of suffering or sickness.

Words to feed upon during faith-famines and light's-out dark nights.

This is one reason why the living faith tradition confesses that *the Word of God is living and active* (Hebrews 4:12), and why Jesus pairs the Word of God with eating the bread of life (John 6:35).

Given that, it is important to grasp that silence is not the pinnacle of spiritual maturity because it mutes us. Rather, silence is the fecund depths of spiritual maturity because through the silence an opening unfolds, a space for grace, that enables the Word of God to be spoken to us, to be heard by us and to again create in and through us a deeper connection and relationality. The depths turn us into the ground in which a seed of God's living and active

Word takes root and grows, producing the fruit of wisdom and love in every season (Psalm 1).

It is my experience that the silence is useful only to the extent that the silence kindles God devotion and unites us more keenly and closely to the living Christ. The silence is only as useful as the silence does. As the silence infuses, heals, and empowers us, we discover within an increasing, joyful sense of freedom. We discover a kindred care toward all. We partake in the wholeness of love triumphing over fear and fragmentation. We discover that when the silence kneels to the Word, silence then serves its Lord well. May it be so.

In the beginning when God created the heavens and the earth, the earth was a formless void and darkness covered the face of the deep, while a wind from God swept over the face of the waters. Then God said, 'Let there be light'; and there was light.

Genesis 1:1–3

THE PRAYERS

JANUARY

I begin again.

January, named for Janus of double-faced wisdom.

In these short days and long nights, I look back upon what has been, and I look forward to what might be.

By your Spirit of holy elegance, may I be a far-seeing one. And a thoroughly seen one.

As we attend to the newness of these days, may I also feel their lineage, unbroken in timelessness, flowing together in the ever-present gift of being here now with you, O my God, and with myself, and with one another.

In the silence of the new year, I see the me is a We.

JANUARY 1

God of My Lifetime:

My heart listens in silence, so still and sacred.

In these moments, I recognize your presence, your faithful love.

Day by day, year by year, decade by decade, your voice is voiceless yet never void.

No matter what I've done or been.

No matter what I haven't done or haven't been.

You are with me—always, love starting my life again, in a silence that speaks.

Amen.

■ ■ ■

JANUARY 2

God, Breather of Light:

In the fields of your light, a stage unfolds for the act of a lifetime.

In its stillness, a cast of love, joy, and hope each call to the congregation of listening hearts to awaken, turn, and remember that your light is our life.

I wish for a holy remembering to play the part I've been given with care, attention, and tenderness to your breath breathing in all and everyone.

Amen.

■ ■ ■

JANUARY 3

God of My Journey:

The aim of my life is revealed by choices.

I learn from the past, and from all prior paths.

And I reaffirm my deep wish that no matter what unfolds this day and year, my heart falls easily into Thee.

Amen.

■ ■ ■

JANUARY 4

Holy Spirit of Care and Kindness:

Your patience tends to my unfolding with such detail.

Day by day, I see my life growing deeper toward your way and wisdom.

I feel your care flowing through me toward others.

I see that the most real me is also a we, and the my is really an interwoven Thy.

Amen.

■ ■ ■

JANUARY 5

God of Every Age and Stage of My Life:

Now it is my turn to seek, to feel, to understand, and to share.

Let my faith flourish and endure and contribute to the living legacy of Christian faith, knowledge, and practice.

Amen.

JANUARY 6

God of Epiphany:

I give thanks for all the ways I am supported.

It only takes an illness or an accident to reveal all the ways I am upheld, ways I often take for granted.

Thank you for the epiphanies of humility that remind me to remember you and remember gratitude even before something I cherish is taken away.

Remind me to trust in your name and cherish each moment with each person I love.

Remind me to be awake to the gift of health, especially when sick.

Amen.

■ ■ ■

JANUARY 7

Lord Jesus:

The new year unfolds with surprises.

The fresh feeling of opportunity remains, not yet tempered by time.

As the years and decades pass, knowing you becomes the central thread weaving your love and light into my life more deeply.

Pull the thread, and I am undone. You are my everything.

Amen.

■ ■ ■

JANUARY 8

Most Loving and Gracious, Creator God:

I see to connect. I hear to learn. I touch to feel.

Help me see in others your presence.

Help me hear and listen to your wisdom in every silence and within every word spoken.

Help me feel your presence in every encounter with earth, sky, creature, brother, and sister.

Amen.

JANUARY 9

Hidden Glory, Revealed in Christ:

Teach me the way of love in a world of demands and difficulties.

Your grace pulls these forces up by their roots, knotted around the boulders of fear and wanting.

Change my criticisms into compassion.

Your skin isn't sameness. It is a symphony. You wear everyone.

Amen.

■ ■ ■

JANUARY 10

God beyond Time:

Touch my regrets with acceptance and my hopes with possibility.

Infuse this moment with a will toward attunement to your ways.

Attracted and aimed, my bearing is toward you.

Amen.

JANUARY 11

Beloved:

I bless the radiating rays written across the dawn sky.

I bless all who serve the world in its being and becoming today.

And I bless the light of love which helps us all see and be.

Amen.

■ ■ ■

JANUARY 12

God of Consolation:

Every dawn, every day the hills greet me in the same way. Their stillness and graceful lines speak like a presence. The sun rises and the hills awaken like songs sung by the light.

Their form is hidden in the dark, but with the dawn, the hills slowly reveal themselves to the world.

I see their full sweep, east to west, and I feel your everlasting constancy of love for this earth, and humans everywhere watching the dawn for hope.

I bow to the hills as I would a brother.

I raise my hand toward them, offering gratitude for the gifts I've received this morning, the gift of remembering Thee, Thou, the giver of all the hills and the life that flows under them beyond all time.

Amen.

■ ■ ■

JANUARY 13

God, Holy Light:

Awaken me today that I might feel more alive in my body, this vehicle of being here, sheathed as it is in food, breath, thought, will, self, and spirit.

With hands pressed together at my heart, I bow to Thee, giver of this great honor, this deep gift, of being here now.

Amen.

■ ■ ■

JANUARY 14

O God, Deep Cloud of Knowing:

The silence in my heart releases the light of wordless wisdom. And I am at peace.

The stillness holds me calmly, and, in this rest, I see wisdom's light, illuming every question and easing every concern. And I am at peace.

Simplicity and stillness release my fears and ease my questions. And I am at peace.

Amen.

■ ■ ■

JANUARY 15

God, Source of Beauty:

O God, silence brings the sensation of presence.

Silence is the little death.

My personality grows passive. My body grows still. My awareness grows one-pointed toward the warmth of an overflowing heart, in, for, with love for you and all. It is so beautiful to live and feel this way. May your silence be my life.

Amen.

■ ■ ■

JANUARY 16

God, Always Here and Everywhere:

When my heart is heavy carrying life concerns, I turn toward the silence, and there, I remember your Presence is always lifting me up.

In the heaviness of life, you are my still strength.

Amen.

■ ■ ■

JANUARY 17

God, Our Trinity:

O Trinity, I love Thy trinities!

Faith. Hope. Love.

Jesus. Scripture. Community.

Father. Son. Spirit.

Creator. Redeemer. Sanctifier.

Yes. No. Perhaps.

Joseph. Mary. Jesus.

Height. Depth. Breadth.

Transcendence. Imminence. Omnipresence.

All such ways of feeling, knowing, and being minister to me in the Word, Gospel, and goodness of truth, wisdom, and understanding. I eat, drink, and delight in these hymns, songs, and spiritual harmonies that order, nourish, and inspire the light-filled universe of all who ask, seek, and knock at the door of Thy threefold glory, goodness, and dominion.

Amen.

■ ■ ■

JANUARY 18

God, Our Day:

The mid-winter morning light calms the earth with a rose blanket on the eastern sky, where I look with open eyes halfway through my silence. Perhaps I now hear you saying in the space between my closed eyes and open heart:

I care for you. For all of you. I wish for your well-being.

Sense me in your stillness. Feel me in your silence. Know me in your seeing.

Together, we shape the journey of a day and a lifetime. Rosy dawn to violet dusk.

Amen.

■ ■ ■

JANUARY 19

God, My Light and Inspiration:

Your word meets me in the dark dawn and speaks to me in the still silence.

I hear you in the center of my in-breath, here, where I with reverence place my hand upon my chest.

I gently receive an impression, a tenderness. A truth so alive it jolts my body, and the gentle gift of tears flows.

Imprinted in my heart is a lifetime of listening for and to your word, and the listening becomes the presence I seek.

In being with you, I am courageous to be with others, and to be me.

Amen.

■ ■ ■

JANUARY 20

God of Light:

In your light I see the life I lead and remember my ways of being what I have been. I see and understand the history I've created and feel both rebuked and quickened in my spirit. I feel called to live more alive, more joyful, more in faith.

Free me from past patterns of negativity and self-pity that only keep me from connection with friends and disconnected from possibilities outside my daily routines and comforts.

You show me myself in your light so that in Christ, I can be more by being less of myself.

Amen.

JANUARY 21

God, Beloved Horizon:

There is a far hill to the north of my window. At sunrise, it is soaked in shadow. Its expanse, tree covered. No building in sight. This hill keeps my heartstrings connected to even deeper worlds, farther away to the north. Those hills are with me now, as I wish to enter the fellowship of the Son— Christ Jesus. And to feel this Son light the fire of my heart again and renew me with the beauty of being a quiet haven, untouched by the crowded life I daily must tend to. Help me remember the fellowship of the forest and the sun and the trees that are transformed into crosses and the deaths that are lifted up by the sunrise into life.

Amen.

■ ■ ■

JANUARY 22

Holy Trinity of Ever-Expanding Love:

We unfurl this lifetime together. You, with your silence and you with your wisdom and you with your long views. Me, with my questions and me with my unknowing and me with my short views.

I learn so much by looking back to see the choices and contours of this lifetime. It is humbling. There is a balm in simply remembering. I pray now, knowing the past, yet not knowing more than that and knowing this now, to experience the gift of knowing you—beyond what I know about myself.

Amen.

■ ■ ■

JANUARY 23

Spirit of the Living God:

To the earth I kneel this dawn and then lay down my belly and touch my forehead to the ground. I feel my heartbeat against the earth. I feel the cool grass upon my cheek. A stillness arises in my body. My breathing slows. I feel reverence everywhere. I feel surrender in everything. I feel I am yours.

O Spirit of God, anoint me with your wisdom for every choice and patience for every waiting and peace for every stressor and joy for every encounter. Fill this prostration with the power of your risen love.

Amen.

JANUARY 24

God, My Source:

My body remembers moments at ease, comforted by the beauty of sea and sun. The calm of breath quietly moving my belly warmed by the fire beside which I sit.

The embodied journey is the chariot of Thy Spirit, and you walk with us through the seasons. Appointed for our span of breath on this earth, birth to death, we are quickened to breathe your life in deeply, to feel, to experience, to worship, to love.

You are with us in these bodies, as these bodies, no matter their state, shape, or style—we feel your love now.

Amen.

■ ■ ■

JANUARY 25

Giver of New Life:

The gravity of the past and its choices and consequences pulls on my life today. I feel its weight. Yet the grace of your future gives me wings to soar beyond what has been and cast into the discovery of what can be. Your new possibilities of freedom and flight lifting me above the tendrils of time, writing a new name into my heart, declaring a new victory upon the fields of failure that now cease their condemnations, but witness in silence the new, risen me.

Amen.

■ ■ ■

JANUARY 26

Beloved Grace Unending:

I find within this silence an understanding that illumines the shadows of doubt, and though the questions remain, I am different amidst them. And like Job, I feel alive to a different dimension of myself, named peace.

Amen.

■ ■ ■

JANUARY 27

God, My Foundation:

Blessed be the gray sky and the winter day, and all life it foretells of coming showers and wildflowers, and sunlight carpeting the earth.

Blessed be the songs we sing out loud or silently in our breasts, that foretell the coming hymns to Christ, the risen one, through the strife and the tears shed beside the garden of life—the silent place where all things grow and go, where we learn to say "Thy will be done." Though we are yet in winter, it shall be spring.

Amen.

■ ■ ■

JANUARY 28

God, Ground of My Journey:

Change me by what I receive and change me by what I give. And change what I give with all I receive. Furrow deep into my heart, and when I may receive the word that can become life and the life that becomes light, may I hear it and come home to you.

Amen.

JANUARY 29

Joy of My Heart:

This day greets me with breath, breathing me.

Life, living me.

May this lifetime be for letting go more into Thee, both losing myself in Christ and discovering myself in Christ. May union flourish everywhere, harmonized by love.

Amen.

■ ■ ■

JANUARY 30

God of Wholeness:

Amidst any difficulty or pain, I wish to remember I am a part of the wholeness unfolding by the power of your love. May this moment become more aware and filled with peace. May this occasion arise as a mirror, revealing not just myself, but myself in Christ, the body of life for us all.

Amen.

Light of the World:

Lead me from sensing to feeling,

From feeling to thinking,

From thinking to knowing,

From knowing to understanding,

And from understanding to wisdom.

May these dark and most quiet winter days of the year give space for rest and renewal and fill my life with the light of Christ.

Amen.

FEBRUARY

Earth's silence under the snow;
sky's heavy-laden northern clouds
descending.

Still winter holds me as I grow.

I press into the early dark light, with
a candle and a chant.

Something feels like childhood, that
morning just before putting on the
woolen cap and mittens.

Memories of sitting fireside, mother beside me, hot cocoa mug in hand.

Now, decades past, this child's hands pressed together in prayer at the heart, filled with earth's sweet silence.

And mother's grace.

FEBRUARY 1

God, My Strong Foundation:

Holy the steps each day I take toward love.

Holy the breaths each moment I breathe with you, on this way.

Holy the depths I fathom in each prayer I pray.

Amen.

■ ■ ■

FEBRUARY 2

Word of Healing Power:

The shadow of your Word lingers in my heart.

Its edge is soft, yet it cuts me deeply with the grain, yet no pain.

Other than the pain of letting go in surrender.

Amen.

■ ■ ■

FEBRUARY 3

Beloved Lord Jesus Christ, Living Word in My Heart:

No darkness, no shame, no guilt or pain can separate my heart from the light of your name.

Silently, still, and mountain strong, Lord Jesus Christ, Son of God, have mercy on me.

Amen.

■ ■ ■

FEBRUARY 4

God, Breath of this Body:

Unfurl, uncoil, release the peace of your presence in every cell of my existence this day.

Flow through my life and let my words be anointed by your wisdom.

Arise through my body and let my weight be uplifted by your tender mercies.

Grow through my being here now and let my lifetime be crowned with love's gentle victory.

Amen.

FEBRUARY 5

God, Our Light:

Your hiddenness in this season of suffering is not absence.

Even here, even now in this difficulty, I find a nest of rest, and a space for grace, in the silence of your nearness.

Your light is everywhere, even in the darkness.

Amen.

■ ■ ■

FEBRUARY 6

Birther of the Cosmos, Giver of This Day:

Your being is not my being, but your being is my life.

And in this life is a hiddenness.

And in the hiddenness, there is a hearing.

And in the hearing, there is a knowing.

And in the knowing, there is an understanding.

And in the understanding, there is a silence.

And in the silence, there is a feeling.

And in the feeling, there is your being.

And in your being, there is my life.

Amen.

■ ■ ■

FEBRUARY 7

Lord Jesus, Son of Mary:

Draw my hearing to your wisdom that I might take rest from the noise of now, drawn into the depths of eternity's silence.

There, in that still moment, I am touched by the wonder of your presence among us, at once tender child of the mother and sovereign light of every heart.

Amen.

■ ■ ■

FEBRUARY 8

Abba, Beloved Source:

Help me see in every death the flower of life.

I take refuge in the Arc of the Cross, grounded in a mountain of mercy.

And in this Arc, I shall journey till it strikes its beam upon the round stone of resurrection.

In the Arc of the Cross, I find the way through death, and its breath of surrender back to Abba.

Amen.

■ ■ ■

FEBRUARY 9

My God, Thy Grace:

I enter a holy remembering. This moment, this breath, my body recollects your word still writing its remedy into my listening. I lift my arms outstretched with the trees in the winter wind, and I receive your wisdom. This earnest heart, guided gently by your Spirit, a holy remembering that makes the Scriptures sing again.

Amen.

■ ■ ■

FEBRUARY 10

God of My Very Breath:

Your silence circles my life, a gray unknown, a vast territory.

It opens my seeing. It deepens my hearing.

In the emptiness, I am known.

You keep encircling me, a searching horizon moving ever deeper.

Doubt's ledge revealing my journey's surrender, kneeling into a quiet praise.

Praised be the silent God whose Word speaks like wind over the prairie.

Ceaseless is your stillness, this way of words spoken into the wind of remembrance at the ledges.

Amen.

FEBRUARY 11

God of Tender Love and Strong Mercy:

Your tenderness is a herald of eternity.

Your mercy is a healer of time.

May your tender mercy untie the knots tied tight over the years and seasons of my life.

And set me free from the self that forgets you are here now.

Amen.

■ ■ ■

FEBRUARY 12

Holy Spirit, Reconciling Presence:

Attend to the tender wounds where love has collapsed into fear.

We trust your gentle power will weave together oppositions frozen apart.

Arise in my life and my beloveds.

Be the silent key that unlocks the doors slammed shut
between us.

Amen.

■ ■ ■

FEBRUARY 13

Holy the Threefold Name of God:

Praise, God Creator.

Praise, Christ the Living One.

Praise, Holy Spirit God indwelling.

Praise, Holy Trinity, in all and everything.

Amen.

■ ■ ■

FEBRUARY 14

God of My Vows:

To love I am bound. Not by burden, but by the light vow of
consent to be yours, now and always.

Help me keep my vows that bind me to your love, no matter what seeks to distract my attention from your way, in everything I do and everyone I see.

Amen.

■ ■ ■

FEBRUARY 15

Lord Jesus Christ, Way of Life:

Your word fastens to me and holds me as I grow.

May this Lenten journey hold me fast to the grace that flows through your living way.

Let it be a fastening.

A grace that holds fast despite the contradictions my life places against your word and way.

Amen.

■ ■ ■

FEBRUARY 16

My God, Light beyond the Depths:

In the freedom of solitude, school my heart to choose love.

In the energy of silence, shape my love to choose service.

In the peace of simplicity, turn my service into a mercy.

Amen.

■ ■ ■

FEBRUARY 17

Giver of Life, Ground of My Being:

I am the shadow in the light of your praise.

Your heat burns away my inconsistencies.

Your light shows me the possibilities.

Grow a new season in my heart, and let the light consume me.

Amen.

■ ■ ■

FEBRUARY 18

Holy Spirit of God:

The edges of your search fall deep over the world of movement.

Your stillness reaches into the heart of matter, deeper than gravity. Farther than light.

You move with slow strength, a glory condensed into breath.

I am marked by your way of grace.

Your light touch, still upon me like tender morning dew.

Amen.

■ ■ ■

FEBRUARY 19

Light of the World beyond the Dawn:

Be my stillness when I feel flooded with fears.

Be my courage when I feel overwhelmed by all that remains to be done.

Be my everything when I feel I have nothing.

Amen.

FEBRUARY 20

Grace of Jesus, Gentleness of Mary:

Together, you are the company of heaven.

You fashion in my heart the way of faith.

And lead me by remaining beyond my seeing.

Amen.

■ ■ ■

FEBRUARY 21

God of the Healing Hours:

Deep in the soil of darkness, and far into the body of pain, your care is sown like a fire without heat, a cleansing, a rain of light.

Your stillness whispers through the decades; I see their gentle imprints everywhere.

I am furrowed deep by the tracks of your quiet work.

Amen.

FEBRUARY 22

God of My Heart's Repose:

I have wandered long paths nowhere, intrigued by the unknown, enchanted by the mysterious.

I have thought I could find a different way, a more enlightened path, an escape from all that seems foolish in the footsteps of Jesus and the wordy confusions of creed and church.

Now, decades later, and wearied by the search, I find myself returning home where I began, free of the quest, and quiet in simple understanding.

Perhaps all our searching is needed to teach us you have already found us.

The efforts, the questing, and all the unanswered questions make this simple homecoming all the sweeter.

In all my seeking, in the end, the truth isn't knowledge, the truth is a relationship.

Amen.

■ ■ ■

FEBRUARY 23

Bloomer of the Universe:

When I look upon the sweep of the starry night, or the bare limbs of a deep and old, bare forest.

And when I hear the laughter of children playing and see the violet crown of a winter dusk;

I feel that it is all akin to Thee and me, and that we are a part of the universe's tree of life—blooming all around us, we in it and it in us.

And you, O Living God our Creator, are its breather, its bloomer, its tending force.

Amen.

■ ■ ■

FEBRUARY 24

Giver of This New Day:

I stand unencumbered in the company of silence, freed from past doubts and clothed with your far-nearness. The uplift of your presence turns my downcast into devotion. Though

I lack wings to fly, I have the capacity to fall to my knees in worship.

Amen.

■ ■ ■

FEBRUARY 25

Source of Joy through a Lifetime:

Praise be to the spoken one; your word pervades all dim wonderings with the sweetness of seeing.

Praise be to the freeing one; your silence is alive with listening, a repose for my healing.

Praise be to the waiting one; your patience births all being and becoming.

A new day. A new way. A new life.

Amen.

■ ■ ■

God, Source of Life:

As the bud gives way to flower,

And flower gives way to fruit,

And fruit gives way to seed,

And seed gives way to sprout,

And sprout gives way to stem,

And stem gives way to bud,

So too I trust your life and Word will flourish in me—

today, tomorrow, and throughout my timeline.

Amen.

■ ■ ■

FEBRUARY 27

God, Union of Love and Truth:

Lead me to the courage to draw close to the fire of love and the embers of truth.

I do not wish to live a safe distance from the heat of love and the light of truth.

I wish to sit beside the burning circle and become a participant in the fellowship of the consumed.

Amen.

■ ■ ■

FEBRUARY 28

Mind of Christ, Thought of Heaven:

Guide the gaze of my attention and the direction of my focus.

I aim to journey deeper in the reframing insights of your way and wisdom.

Let my consciousness today become a temple for your expression,

A particular place of radiance amidst the whole realm of your healing endeavor.

Amen.

■ ■ ■

FEBRUARY 29 (LEAP YEAR)

God of the Whole and Healer of the Peace:

Reclaim in me an expanse of peace, where the knowing substance of my soul can rejoice in its peaceful homecoming from all the distress amidst an agitated culture.

Amen.

MARCH

It is as if God says to me:

I am the soft imprint in your soul.

I am the shadow cast by love.

I am the tender impression left by the sea upon the roving inner shore.

Let's grow deeper together.

MARCH 1

Spirit of the Peace of God:

Let me take rest in the stillness and know that you are God.

This is a season of transition. Shifts are occurring all around me. Relationships are strained.

Lead me to a rest that is deeper than my capacities to find on my own.

Amen.

■ ■ ■

MARCH 2

Spirit of Possibility:

Let me take hope in waiting upon your presence.

Your living Word strengthens my heart even as I perceive discouraging events.

Lead me to this hope that is broader than my capacities to see on my own.

Amen.

MARCH 3

Spirit of Power:

Let me take strength in Christ through whom every vulnerability can be transformed into a tool for understanding.

Your strength is the paradoxical power of surrender. The might of letting go and letting be.

Lead me to this strength that is higher than my capacities to sustain on my own.

Amen.

■ ■ ■

MARCH 4

Spirit of New Beginnings:

Align with wisdom the decisions that have gone sideways.

Anoint with peace the deals that have turned conflicted.

Allow abundance to arise from the choices that have led to losses.

Amen.

MARCH 5

Abba, Father:

The earth is bearing witness to the upsurge of new life, attentive to the light of the sun.

Winter is completing, even if the soil lays quiet and still frozen. Everything is saying yes to growing again.

Like the earth, I await the slow process of quickening toward your depth and height, your heated ground and holy Son.

Amen.

■ ■ ■

MARCH 6

Ever Far-Nearness of Tender Mercies:

Attend to the seams of sadness running deep through the foundation of my heart.

Underneath the sadness are fragments of unmet desires and thwarted dreams.

Help me hold this sadness with tenderness, like a long-lost friend come home.

I follow the sadness into the first desires and understand that sadness is not the problem, it is the fruit of desire, and the sadness shows me where I can place my efforts and lift up my intentions with perhaps a stronger force for what is truly in my heart.

And consent to your mercy for all results.

Amen.

■ ■ ■

MARCH 7

My Refuge:

This quivering consciousness at the edge of its knowing finally is all aflame, but unconsumed.

My life is a holy bush, a witness to your temple, a tincture of your Spirit's fire.

Like a drop of light on the horizon, I train my inner eye to see beyond the edge of darkness and follow you into the deserted spaces of overwhelming silence so to hear again for the first time, and to be heard from the crying place.

Amen.

MARCH 8

God of the Mountain Encounter:

Your revelations give me more than I can bear.

You are a vastness that can't be explained, yet deeply felt.

An openness of space that unfurls time into timelessness.

An everlasting listening.

A wordless speaking.

And the clouds of my soul part to you.

Amen.

■ ■ ■

MARCH 9

Holy Rootedness of My Life:

Your silence is my continuance and constancy through the dark night of life's unexpected turns.

I feel the rootedness of your ever-faithful love growing within me.

You are the alma mater of my lifetime, and I return again and again to you, remembering who I have wished to become.

Amen.

■ ■ ■

MARCH 10

God of the Open Door:

Let the bright edge of Lent cut away the dim-hearted callouses of fear and regret that cover the doorways of my life leading to new freedom and joy.

Give me the courage to walk through the open door in front of me instead of analyzing why other doors remain shut.

Amen.

■ ■ ■

MARCH 11

Christ, Emptied to Fill:

Teach me the way of the zero—a powerful emptiness, a profound nothing, a mediating space that holds everything together without being anything but its open self to you.

In a world of accumulation and assertions of being somebody, teach me the way of the zero. The way of the kenotic Christ. The way of reconciliation, bridging the gap between the negative and positive dynamics of life.

Amen.

■ ■ ■

MARCH 12

Heart-Rending Beauty:

Green grass of the field kneeling before the tall, Atlantic forest.

Wind hears itself through the young leaves drenched in an afternoon of tender rain.

Can you hear this anywhere else—the sound of peace, the sound of homecoming—young leaves discovering the first love of wind's caress?

I am made for the wind. I am here to be moved by its force and feel the joy of being moved in its rhythms.

Amen.

■ ■ ■

MARCH 13

God of Remembrances:

Holy the delight in pondering.

Holy the goodness in remembering.

My life opens like a book; well-turned pages mark moments I cherish and some I chide.

They dwell within me, and I dwell within them.

Time is a tense keeper—been, being, become. I take flight from time in memory, and all things converge together in a silent sapphire moment, suspended by the powers of memory, and distilled in the saline of my tears, shed to the earth: time becoming feeling, becoming a chemical reaction of my body returning to the body of the earth.

Amen.

■ ■ ■

MARCH 14

God, Unbounded Center:

I follow the narrow line of time unfolding with a patient leaning toward what is yet to be.

I live holding a gentle waiting in my cupped hands, breathing the breath of faith to unveil its next moves. And you wait with me.

Amen.

■ ■ ■

MARCH 15

God of New Turnings:

Silence is stronger than the words inside me wishing to be spoken.

You lead me to turn the other cheek, to remain silent and still.

You are the first dawn in me of the nonreactive self, the me that is hidden with you in Christ.

Amen.

■ ■ ■

MARCH 16

Christ, the Descended One:

The night of angst buries me in its crashing waves.

And as I roll in its thundering weight, a word of light descends to me and lifts me up through the solitude of this Lenten purging.

A word that saves me from the harrowing encounter with emptiness at the edge of oceanic questions.

Amen.

■ ■ ■

MARCH 17

Christ, Bread of Life:

Through the storm, I hear your word of commitment. It is like the dark, deep ground holding the ancient oak, shaking in the sheering wind.

It is a word that can't be spoken or shared.

It is a word that can be cut open; a word to be eaten by the half-broken mind, relieved to find itself fed again by a whole-making truth.

Amen.

■ ■ ■

MARCH 18

God of Liberating Grace:

On this Lenten way, help me stand in the truth and certainty of forgiveness.

Help me make an enduring avowal of all remorse and regret.

And to live following the leadership of possibility not being pushed by the bully of past regrets.

Amen.

■ ■ ■

MARCH 19

God of the New Covenant:

Tears of joy blur into silent praise, standing in wonder at the "I" that feels the harmony of the universe kneeling to the holy name, and rising to attention in the grace of Christ's feast of self-giving.

My heart is ablaze to remember the torment turned triumph.

Amen.

MARCH 20

All Knowing and Loving God of My Heart:

I await your understanding, as the shore awaits the tide.

May your wisdom take out to the sea of forgetfulness all ideas that only clutter my heart with the debris of doubt. I wish to live by the cadences of your faithfulness and keep to the hours of encouragement, letting the days of confusion slip forever away.

Amen.

■ ■ ■

MARCH 21

Eternal Name beyond All Names:

In the name of the hushed ancient forest.

In the name of the cresting hills and out-stretching prairies.

In the name of the starry night overcasting silent and still fields of dreams.

In the name of the granite mountains raising their ridges against the midnight sky.

In the name of the shadowed sea upon which I cross this night of agony.

I live and speak as a named one—and in naming my inner memories, I come to life more fully in your story of creation and redemption.

Amen.

■ ■ ■

MARCH 22

Jesus, Voice Drawing All Disciples:

In your Name above all names, I am given a share in the universe and a part of the whole.

My heart knows its calling because it is foremost a called and named one.

And my heart follows you by praising your Name.

Amen.

MARCH 23

Christ Jesus, Word of God:

Your life bore the wounding words of empire and emperors.

You are the wounded Word.

Yet your words never wound. Your words bind the broken, heal the sick, and raise the dead.

You are our wounded, healing Word.

You are the wounded Word that bled the Book of Life into being.

You are the wounded Word, and, in your wounds, we find a womb to new life.

Amen.

■ ■ ■

MARCH 24

Light of Light, Life of Life:

All praise be to you, O radiant creator of all that is.

You have gifted us with the pleasures of this domain and charged us with a regency of care.

All mercy and grace to us, for the worlds that we make and break.

All justice and remediation for the shattered landscapes we have left in pursuit of our various powers and profits. Lord, have mercy.

Amen.

■ ■ ■

MARCH 25

God of All Galaxies, Planets, and Stars:

The wind keeps speaking to us. The forest trees are ceaseless in their leafy song.

The earth grows fierce in its reprisal for us to courageously take care now and for the future.

Pacific fields sway with sapphire-blue limpidity, listening to me as I listen to it. The sea watching me, as I watch it.

Amen.

MARCH 26

Christ, Liberator from All Regrets:

Teach me that all my feelings of regret and remorse are good for but a second.

Show me how to let them pin me down just for a second, so to teach me something fierce, if need be.

Then release them by the power of your forgiveness. And your grace will lead me to the font of forgetfulness.

Give me the courage to spend no energy trying to undo what has been.

Let me meet the moment more aware, more effective now because of the past, which is a teacher and guide, not my master.

Help me see how the future is drawing me forward. Unlike the past, my future is not filled yet. It is empty. Give me the presence of mind to not fill it with regret. Rather, to fill it with possibility and prayerful wondering, courageous action, imagination, and creativity.

Amen.

■ ■ ■

MARCH 27

Lord of Gethsemane's Trees:

As I walk through the vulnerabilities of life, I read the vernal forest for signs and insights.

I listen carefully for guidance and gumption to dream wider dreams and speak the wishes of my heart into the wind.

The forest accompanies me on this journey, and the tall, rooted trees give to me courage from their spiraled seasons of growth.

Amen.

■ ■ ■

MARCH 28

Lord of Golgotha's Cross:

You join me at the edge of my despair with your own tears for the way the world is. I kneel to join you in your sorrows, so to breathe, as if one breath, with your final cry to the Father.

Amen.

MARCH 29

Lord of the Holy Triduum:

I've lived enough to feel the gist of life's hazards and holiness.

Now, I wish to feel the hymn of crucifixion and the anthem of resurrection.

And sing their darkness and light into the logic of my every perception and the pathos of my every feeling, now and always.

Amen.

■ ■ ■

MARCH 30

Lord of the Last Supper:

Your upper room words are the coordinates that orient my life. Abiding in your promises is the only truth that absorbs my disorientation and reorientates everything in my life into your story.

Amen.

MARCH 31

Lord of the Resurrection:

A mighty joy is my strength. A buoyancy never failing.

Your resurrection life is the emblem of victory over all fears and curses against the power of love.

In your life I live.

Amen.

APRIL

It is as if the Spirit says:

Again, my grace greets you with this new month, this new day.

I am with you always. There is no accounting of my faithfulness.

It is vast beyond measure, and surprisingly generous.

Call to me with your tears, with your words, with your silence, with your body—and I will advance your vision to see me more clearly in whatever might be arising. And this seeing will be a freeing to you.

APRIL 1

Holy Spirit of Transformation:

Your work of grace arises like a loving vastness that I can't explain. I feel its warmth beyond the edges of myself.

And sometimes it is as if your vastness distills into a dew drop of presence anointing my heart with devotion.

Amen.

■ ■ ■

APRIL 2

God of Beginnings and Endings:

Eternity lies dormant in my soul. And the beauty of the earth, the wisdom of your Word, and the goodness of human relating all awaken the connection that weaves me into your great beyond.

And time spreads itself over the matrix of my life with through lines, worn channels where memory and hope may flow. I welcome this facticity of time and rejoice in its pages, which allow my book of life to be written and remembered.

Amen.

APRIL 3

Holy Wisdom:

Your Word evokes the gift of repentance.

Your Word rebukes with gentle power to heal with powerful gentleness.

Have mercy upon my hesitation to give back to others and my quick willingness to get or take just for myself.

Amen.

■ ■ ■

APRIL 4

Spirit of Divine Favor:

Your mercy gives rise to hope, and your hope finds a way to move through closed doors and see around blind spots. Be my companion today: my heart is listening.

Amen.

■ ■ ■

APRIL 5

Jesus, Keeper of the Night Vigil:

I hear the words of Holy Week echoing in the heart of memory: *stay with me, watch with me, pray with me.* I have no excuse, yet I wander. I complain. I drift to sleep.

May this season of new life infuse my heart with a new and deepened attraction to stay, watch, and pray.

Amen.

***

APRIL 6

Jesus, Brother to All Who Suffer:

You are the stillness that wraps itself in the dark torrent of violence, joining our human journey into pain and seeming godforsakenness.

Your cross is communicating a chosen powerlessness in the face of human forgetfulness of the ways of love.

I am listening to the rage against such ways growing quietly in my heart.

And I am trying to follow your way of silence and consent.

Amen.

Jesus, Son of God:

You are the timely fullness of remedy in the abyss of my need.

Your refuge extends to every human weakness, as a tireless rescue from the burden of shame and the contortions of guilt.

Amen.

■ ■ ■

APRIL 8

All and Everything, Thrice Holy Art Thou Creator:

I am a particle of the exhaled breath of creation, one among billions who consummate your desire for there to be something and not nothing.

Your life is breathing all into being and the memory of your Son among us is a myrrh to my mind.

Amen.

APRIL 9

God, My God:

You are the Spirit of aliveness itself. The growing of growth. The green of life. The farness of transcendence. The nearness of imminence. The holy of holiness burning sacred fires that blaze without consuming. You are like the grit of sand on my skin.

And yet you also spread your banquet in the dark, cleansing desert.

Your absence chafes my body.

Your presence cracks my mind.

Your Word pierces my heart.

I am wounded by it all, and I grow young again, leaking everything my "I" has fashioned and fastened to in my own image.

You abandon me again so that "I" can be found by the wider I now not I, but Christ in me.

Amen.

■ ■ ■

APRIL 10

God of New Life:

You are the new wine that shines in my heart with a candor and courage like a fresh rain after a long drought.

Your truth tends toward goodness, and your goodness bends beauty into everything.

And this harmony, this trinity of truth-goodness-beauty is everything to a praise-full heart and voice. I can't help but voice forth my praises in song and dance with up-stretched arms and hands to heaven.

Amen.

■ ■ ■

APRIL 11

Living Waters of Loving-kindness:

I feel alive in the flood of remembrance, flowing me into an era of gratitude and a new season of possibility.

Your grace leads me like a river to the edge of a high and heavy waterfall. Will I survive the plunge? What is around the big bend? Where will the river take me? What will the water reveal? Can I drink of the very flow that takes me into the unknown?

Yes, for you are the headwaters and the great delta greeting the sea.

Amen.

■ ■ ■

APRIL 12

Cascading Consummations of Angelic Praise:

Your radiant name of sanctity was breathed into eternity and took flesh in time to reveal itself for our healing from the curse of forgetting your name and not knowing our own.

Your name is written with light deeper than words and softer than silence.

You are the living Jesus Christ, Son of the Living God, ever born, ever the manifestation of the holy unknown of Abba's image for the universe to see and recognize that you are the progenitor of all who participate in the field and form of energy, matter, life, thought, and feeling.

Amen.

APRIL 13

God of Resurrection Power:

Your heart of care kneels to water the earth with your holy tears of tender mercies.

A gentle stream of wisdom cracks open my too long unsung heart, absent and unaccounted for, far away on its own endeavors.

The pain of recognizing my lostness is brief, yet in the shards of repentance, a voice of rebuke is heard, silently signing a new heavens and earth into my heart, lifting me toward your breath as you raise me by your oceanic grace.

Amen.

■ ■ ■

APRIL 14

Risen Lord of the Seed of Adam:

Chance is unlucky and providence is crafty. Crazed are the seeing ones who think they see you in the darkness of illumination. And tipsy are the learned ones who think they know.

But blessed are the humbled ones instructed by the stillness of simplicity. These are the family of the meek who shall inherit the gentle reign of faith's victory and be Christ's bride.

Amen.

■ ■ ■

APRIL 15

Holy Center of the Cloud of Witnesses:

I am a sung one. And the song sings me.

Its hallelujah fills every breath of my being-here-nowness and conducts me into the harmony of the Body of Christ's choir of praise.

Amen.

■ ■ ■

APRIL 16

God of the First and Last Talent:

Let my wealth be known and measured by the scales of love, where every ounce given away becomes a pound of treasure.

And every ledger is turned upside down so that forgiveness pours out upon all debts and debtors, now set free, endowed with laughter and joy.

Help me live by the laws of abundance, not the contractions of greed.

Amen.

■ ■ ■

APRIL 17

God of Multiplying Effect:

Bless all people with an ample flow of provision and the joy of abundant, overflowing supply.

Transform every concern of scarcity and separation into generous hospitality.

Liberate us from our useless acting out from fear and help us all live by the new economy of nurturing others into unexpected blessings.

Amen.

■ ■ ■

APRIL 18

God of Triune Revelation:

You cross my life with your Holy Name of love. The names run like seams over my being: God Transcendent Source. God the Living One, Spirit the indwelling, tending teacher.

Amen.

■ ■ ■

APRIL 19

Overshadowing Holy Spirit:

You are teaching me the way of strong adoration in the shade of Mary's mercy.

You are reminding me that Mother Mary is the care of God roving through the human family, with ease, generosity, and attention to the little footprints all of God's children make on their journey from being lost to returning home, safe and found.

Amen.

■ ■ ■

APRIL 20

Spirit of Reconciling Peace:

Tame the challenge anger makes to my peaceful heart.

Ease envy's burn and release greed's toothy grip.

Set me free to bear the fruit of your Spirit, in all their ripe fullness.

Amen.

■ ■ ■

APRIL 21

Jesus, the Christ, Ever Abiding in Abba:

I bear witness at the edge of Jesus's union, human and divine, to the holy mystery at the heart of the incarnation.

You, Lord Jesus, are the vast speech of God. The pattern of Abba's heart in human form. The eternal and before all time, wisdom and quantum knowing. The form of all forms fashioning all and everything into the unfolding being of the universe and beyond, in, through, and as divine speech.

You have revealed yourself as the Son Jesus, not to teach us about all the glory you possessed prior to your birth among us, but more so to show us that all that glory is now known for all time as the humble, human Son of Man, Jesus, our Lord.

Amen.

■ ■ ■

APRIL 22

Lord Jesus Christ:

I stand in awe of your human nature, and your ways of gentle embrace of the stranger and the sick.

I stand in awe of your divine nature, and your enigmatic powers that confront darkness and the work of the devil's fear and deception.

In one person, as the mode of the Son, one with the Father and the Spirit, your substance changed the story of the universe, and the book of earth, and every sentence of every human life.

How can I not worship you?

Amen.

APRIL 23

Anointing Holy Spirit:

Your presence in my life is like the gentle, cool rain this early spring day.

Its qualities of quietness and clarity evoke your simple waiting upon me to ask, seek, and knock for the way to be opened to deeper wisdom and faithful love.

Anoint my life with *humilitas*. Crown my life with *gravitas*. And flow through my life with heavenly *hilaritas*, that unmistakable joy of the Lord that is my strength.

Amen.

■ ■ ■

APRIL 24

Risen Morning Light:

You shall awaken praise in those who see—

with faith's eyes,

light's presence

in and through all things.

Risen morning light,

you shall praise every word spoken,

greeting this dawn's silence,

with love's warmth and faith's possibilities.

Amen.

■ ■ ■

APRIL 25

Source of My Strength:

Help me remember that I am held by a deep strength amidst currents that feel as if they are sweeping me over the horizon of safety and certainty.

I am held secure, not by my own strength or cleverness, but by your ever-present embrace.

Amen.

■ ■ ■

APRIL 26

Christ, Our Living Water:

The memory of rain charts through rock, leaving small seams that become streams, then rivers, then oceans.

Rain follows the humble way, the low way, filling hidden places with its life, presence, and power. So too can rain overwhelm, leaving the memory of deluge.

For all who receive too much rain; for all who receive too little rain, I pray for balance and the blessing of Christ as living water for all.

Amen.

■ ■ ■

APRIL 27

Spirit, My Cup-Filler:

Pour into the empty places of my longing the presence of your fulfilling joy.

Overflow my vessel of devotion that lives to feel your flow in and through me.

My body, Thy temple.

My lifetime, Thy breath.

Amen.

■ ■ ■

APRIL 28

Beloved and Faithful Presence:

Where betrayal has broken the trusting place in my heart,

where slander and gossip have punctured my faith in friends—

you are my peaceful solace and steady care after the tumult of every relational rupture.

Amen.

■ ■ ■

APRIL 29

God, My Source of Seeing:

Help me remember you are the light even when the muse of my mind seems to fail and dim.

Even then, your light can and will live in and through me as creative inspiration.

Let every song I sing, every dance I move, every word I speak and write, and every craft I shape, be a witness to your continuing creation.

Amen.

■ ■ ■

APRIL 30

Creator God of the Earth:

I am enfolded by the green, growing days—

the rising sun farther to the northern line of solstice,

the warmer air,

the cooling rains,

the flowers and fields soaking up the sun.

And I join the earth in listening.

Your silence speaks.

Your word opens my heart to listen and understand the silence of the Son, and I grow.

Amen.

MAY

It is as if God says:

I am hiding as joy in the rain of your tears.

Your griefs stream down through the valleys of your years.

And my Gethsemane canyons receive each pearled weeping.

Your tears fill up my cup of care, which I now touch and turn into prayer.

And my tender angels cascade care upon your weeping.

You will soon sing a deeper song, arias arising through grief's deep chasms and dissonant chords.

And a choir of companions in tune with your muted heart will raise songs of remembering.

So you hear heaven voiced in their tears too.

MAY 1

Christ Unbound and Unbinding:

Untie the knots that cinch my heart to fear and past failures.

Unbind the habits that constrict my freedom and joy and keep me contained in tombs of my own making.

I wish to feel the freedom of your touch all over my life and fall into the raiment of ascension.

Amen.

■ ■ ■

MAY 2

Holy Trinity:

You are holy, the affirming.

You are holy, the denying.

You are holy, the reconciling.

I consent this day a bit more of my being here now into the flow of your power, the force of tenderness, and the faithfulness of your love.

Amen.

MAY 3

Light of the World:

Seal the leaks that drain my energy.

Strengthen my will and resolve to keep my sacred aims and not let life deplete me with its petty difficulties, small dislikes, or frictions caused by others' surface personality.

Transform every conflict into a school of love, a furnace of purification, in service to a maturing freedom from self.

Amen.

■ ■ ■

MAY 4

Grace Guiding My Life:

Ambiguities appear at every turn.

I look forward and see uncertainty.

I look backward and see confusion.

I look down and see contradictions.

But when I look up in surrender, grace dissolves my seeing into freeing, and where I can't see clearly, I hear your voice in the silence, deeply calling me to simply trust that you are with me, guiding through it all.

Amen.

■ ■ ■

MAY 5

Christ, Liberator from All Debts:

Your patience frees me from a tendency to make others wrong.

Your humility inspires me to let go of the need to always be right.

Your faith shows me the way to trust the place of powerlessness instead of constantly trying to justify myself.

Amen.

■ ■ ■

MAY 6

God, My Freedom:

Bent by the forces of life, I kneel in consent, asking for help.

I am discovering that every incapacity can also become a liberty.

My inability to do is also an ability to simply be.

I am learning how to let go of my demands for success and surrender to you.

Amen.

■ ■ ■

MAY 7

God of Clarity:

Where I feel confusion, focus my mind on the simplicity of my breath.

Where I feel insecure, expand my heart with the courage that arises when all seems lost.

Where I feel self-doubt, ground my body in the promises of Scripture, reminding me that I belong to you.

Amen.

MAY 8

Unfolding Trinity of Holy Light:

You fathom me with your searching presence.

And I fathom your silence with my tender prayers, sounding out all that confounds.

And I both discover and am discovered by the unfathomable love at the center of all depths and heights.

Amen.

■ ■ ■

MAY 9

God, Giver of This and Every Moment:

I remember past, present, and future with a gentle attention of my awareness. I place my mind and heart into moments past, into this moment, into future moments, and it is as if I can feel and see through the remembering. But most of all I am lifted from the tyranny of time. I awaken more and more to the truth that you remember me, and us, and that your remembering is the energy of love, the very life of the world. And I feel joy.

Amen.

MAY 10

Christ, Brother to My Tears:

Where the brokenness of the world sears my heart into tears, I ask for the freedom to simply weep, not preach. To cry, not speak. To be still, not restless. To be silent, not resentful or reactive.

Amen.

■ ■ ■

MAY 11

Spirit, Hidden Source of Life:

I wait in the silence of your love, and the silence of your love waits in me:

Till my face can speak with softness and care,

Till my words can resonate with warmth and wisdom,

Till my hands can rest in centered calm,

Till silence is all that needs to be.

Amen.

MAY 12

God, Mountain of Presence:

I discover myself as known, opened by the morning light.

The view just over the leafing trees hides the blue northern horizon.

As with faith, I see, but not completely.

As with life, I partake, but only partly.

Hiding through the trees is a range of hills I can't yet see, drawing my attention.

As with faith, you are there too, beyond the veiled green-growing things of life.

You rise, hidden among us at the edges of our knowing.

Amen.

■ ■ ■

MAY 13

Jesus, the Remembered One:

Through the veil of time your life reaches my silent waiting with a word that helps me remember, and in remembering, understand, and in understanding, see clearly.

Remembering you, I remember myself.

I remember my future, and I awake this day more congruent with the possibilities you have placed within my heart.

Amen.

■ ■ ■

MAY 14

God, Faithful Love Holding All Together:

In the space between us, there arises a presence of love.

You hold within your being a distance, a space, a kind of emptiness that welcomes all and everyone.

In this space within yourself, your love greets everything.

I am at home in that distance that is also a nearness.

Amen.

■ ■ ■

MAY 15

Beloved Center:

I feel my heartbeat. I feel my breath. I feel the weight of my body.

This is called being alive and knowing so.

I am held by your distance. I am held by your closeness.

In your infinite center, I am never lost, and I am always known, loved, and discovered.

This discovery helps me cherish the gift of life and enjoy it with others.

We are alive to live.

Amen.

■ ■ ■

MAY 16

Light of My Life:

You are my victory.

Your gentleness crowns me with tender authority and placid strength.

And so anointed and reminded, I move calmly through the stresses of this day.

Amen.

■ ■ ■

MAY 17

Beloved, beyond, in, and through Life:

Pierced by beauty, all things reach me with subtle power and move through my awareness with perfect ease.

So awakened, I find everything is my teacher. And I learn, watching it all become beautiful.

Amen.

■ ■ ■

MAY 18

Trinity, Destination of My Desiring:

Your braided beauty weaves itself into my heart.

And my life upturns toward joy.

Where I was seeking, I am found.

Where I was longing, I am at peace.

A hue from your radiance flows through me, and so this living is now for giving.

Amen.

■ ■ ■

MAY 19

Creating God, Giver of Life:

Your elegant morning graces bidden in the sunlight and shimmering dew are a kind of benevolent force that raises the dead parts of my life into a woven cord of new possibilities.

I lift my hands toward the sky.

I feel my feet upon the earth.

I breathe deeply. I am a part of life itself living through me.

I praise your hidden ways among us.

Amen.

MAY 20

Spirit, Shy Power of the Holy Trinity:

Prairie fields created for wind's pleasure heave down to earth, then up to sky.

The field speaks of your unseen presence—your force is unmistakable.

You are here with us. Together, you weave us into your way by wind.

And your silent streaming guides us forward.

Amen.

■ ■ ■

MAY 21

Christ, Clear Word of the Holy Trinity:

Praise be to the dawn rising, a glory crowning the night.

Your rising is a connecting, all and everything, never the same.

By your rising, Lord Jesus, infuse your Word in us with subtle knowing and generous doing.

Amen.

MAY 22

God, Promise Maker:

Help me with an increasing ability to live with delays without losing faith in your promises.

Let every waiting become a birthing in me of an unshakable foundation of faith.

Help me remember that time isn't just a restriction, it is also a teacher and a blank canvas for shaping my attention and expressing my creative energy.

Amen.

■ ■ ■

MAY 23

Beloved Source of My Ease:

Attend to my heart today.

Speak your words of strengthening.

Let me hear under the noise of life your calming silence.

Let me feel under the full schedule of appointments your peaceful stillness.

Amen.

MAY 24

Healing Presence:

Aligned by the peace given through the silence, I praise your name and lift my heart in continued alertness. I wish to remain in this place of ease.

The sense of self that often feels disconnected recovers its bearings and discovers a relating oneness within everything and everyone.

I am free and connected.

Amen.

■ ■ ■

MAY 25

Giver of the Good, Ground of the Truth, Source of the Beautiful:

Enkindle my empathy to feel the guidance of grace beyond mere expediency.

Expand my perception to understand the wisdom amidst information.

Enliven my senses to recognize the beauty amidst the ordinary.

Amen.

■ ■ ■

MAY 26

Living Spirit of the Verdant Spring:

Joyful inner springs flow to meet the bitterness at the edges of my being.

Your grace gives an agency to rise above, beyond, and through the sorrow life hosts as an all too frequent guest.

I stand ranged about by righteous mountains that draw my attention upward, calling me to kneel in gentle petition, joining their wordless song that tunes with the mourning dove's call, the cascading water's tympani, the pitch and swell of the wind through birch and aspen groves.

Thus, joy.

Amen.

■ ■ ■

Paraclete, My Teacher:

Infuse my sensation with the anointing of your Spirit.

I wish to feel the relating force of your presence in and through me, as I listen for clarity that comes when Spirit articulates the truth through the tempest of opinions.

Amen.

■ ■ ■

MAY 28

Spirit of the Living Christ:

Once misled by my own fears, I lived singed by despair.

But I now live at ease.

My life is centered in a peaceful way, guided by the presence of your unseen silence.

I am reminded by every breath that there is nowhere I can go apart from your Spirit, nowhere you are not with me.

I wish this healing and knowing for all people, everywhere.

May every despair become a turning point, a signal on the horizon of the self, that there is more to life than I can see.

Amen.

■ ■ ■

MAY 29

Transforming Silence:

Your silence shapes the center of my life toward qualities of goodness and peace.

I feel at ease resting in stillness. I feel at peace walking in the forest.

That I am created by you means I am created for you.

Remembering this changes everything.

Amen.

■ ■ ■

MAY 30

Life-Transforming Grace:

Where my impulsivity and hastiness have contributed to what seem to be large mistakes in the story of my life, I find your mercy and grace greeting me and writing new stories with the broken lines of a few torn pages. And I am instructed by such miracles of redeeming. Despite life's sorrows, everything belongs, and everything can become beautiful in its own way.

Amen.

■ ■ ■

MAY 31

Beloved, Heart-Opening Grace:

Opened by the suffering of life, I see new perspectives bigger than the constrained limitations my fears and judgments overlaid upon all past seeing.

Your gentle breaking open of my heart gives me a newfound freedom to see in all and everything not only a softer way of being me, but also a more graceful way toward others' way of being.

Amen.

JUNE

It is as if God says:

I am the field of tenderness growing through every
sorrow that furrows your heart soft.

I am the sunlight that greets your shadowed tears,
counting each with silent care.

I am the listening at rest deep within all your errands
and enduring, saying:

Take and eat this light-filled silence and become
more complete by letting go.

I will carry you through all doubts into the
certainty of my mystery, a generative unknowing
birthing wisdom and fecundity.

JUNE 1

Christ, Bright Dawn of the World:

Cast your clarity into the shadows of doubt that pool upon my thinking and bring your understanding.

Where I feel despair, bring hope.

Where I see suffering, inspire wisdom's best ways to care.

Your flame of Pentecost burns the ashes of transformation into the breath of prayers.

Amen.

■ ■ ■

JUNE 2

Mainstay of My Life:

The middle month of the year uplifts like a ridgepole the tent of time and the arc of the sun. Light reaches its fullness soon and speaks of Christ the Son with silent glory and ascended constancy. This radiance and heat nourish a living world, a green growing, a flourishing.

So too may I grow, fed by the light of Christ.

Amen.

JUNE 3

God, Eden Giver of Trees:

The forest greets me with its green silence and stability. The trees never move or walk or take a journey. They are rooted and only sway when moved by the wind. They reach with branches to the light yet have no hands to grasp. Their leaves never take, yet always receive. The trees don't demand, they bend and bow, and flow with the seasons of the sun's nearness or farness. Winter's cold or summer's heat. Teach me the way of Eden's trees as I journey through life's forest. Even when a tree becomes a cross.

Amen.

■ ■ ■

JUNE 4

Christ, Liberator from the Ways of Empire:

Tender-hearted is this way of silence, this resting turn of head to heart.

Feed the place of courage in me as I move outward beyond ranges of safety—into the unknown, toward places of seeming fierceness and harshness.

Let the strength of your peace be my shield of choice rather than joining in the pointless acting out from fear or ego, adding to the conflagration of enmity.

Your joy is my strength—even if it appears as weakness to others.

Amen.

■ ■ ■

JUNE 5

Lord God, Earth Creator and Tender:

I feel the heavenliness of life in the fullness of dark green pines and hemlocks forested tightly beside a mountain lake, so cold, so clear its water. This heavenly morning is a sign for all the year of the essence of heavenliness here with us, even if just for a brief season. It is enough, Lord, and I feel your heaven here on this earth.

Amen.

■ ■ ■

JUNE 6

All-Seeing Beloved of the Ages:

My eyes face the forest, and the forest faces the sky, and the sky faces your eternity.

We see together and are seen.

Bless this becoming and weave our sight into vision—the far-gazing clarity of love that also cares and creates.

Amen.

■ ■ ■

JUNE 7

God, Beloved Source:

Your reaching grace gently unfolds the clutched places in my heart and opens me to a flowing forgiveness: generous in its measure. Outreaching with kindness. Beautiful in its understanding ways.

Amen.

■ ■ ■

JUNE 8

Eternal Present Here and Now:

The many beguiling choices of this season of life open with ease as I sit in silence listening for the space of vastness to speak its guidance and clarity, like a valley view that appears unexpectedly. The open, empty space makes sense of nearly everything occurring, and it balances the choices with a one-pointed focus toward unmistakable action. I am at ease, and right action becomes clear.

Amen.

■ ■ ■

JUNE 9

Holy Spirit, Home of My Being:

Engraft within me a humble hope to move forward into the maze of our culture's making.

And forge my courage into wisdom as I face the outward world and my relating to it.

Amen.

JUNE 10

God, Light Eternal:

Feeling after you, I seek you through the cloud of my own forgetfulness.

I am grasped by a ray of your alighting wisdom, and you show me the Son, transcending and including everything human. You are ever so close, ever so near. So graced, I remember once again.

Amen.

■ ■ ■

JUNE 11

Spirit of Encircling Peace:

Meanness comes in many forms. The mocking type is especially barbed and difficult to receive.

When caught in the vice of another's forgetfulness of love, help me remember my deeper truths.

Help me see the other's negative attitude as their inner yet-to-be-healed place—not mine to resolve.

What is mine is the invitation to not react with retribution or clam up with frustration—but to stay in the flow of your joy and the depth of your love, centered in a peace-filled silence beyond any words lacking love, kindness, or truth.

Amen.

■ ■ ■

JUNE 12

Jesus of the Cross:

Your name is unyielding truth, a radiating temple encircling all time, all space.

Your truth is a reconciling attunement, easing opposites into generative possibilities.

Your attunement births harmony beyond all contention.

Beauty beyond all critique.

Peace beyond all conflict.

Creation out of chaos.

Amen.

JUNE 13

Creator, Joy of Our Being and Becoming:

There is a seam in the heart of God, in the soft place—a weakness that lets everyone and everything in.

God's holy circumference of infinite love breaks open into a vortex of love, the spiral sphere of creative eros.

And at this broken-open place of possibilities, this tender entrance to the light, the face of the deep cups our tears with gentleness and kisses our sorrows with joy.

Everyone and everything journeys toward this seam in the universe of God.

God is our refuge, our rest, our consummation.

Amen.

■ ■ ■

JUNE 14

God, Place of Peace:

Thank you for the ways I grow strong in the grace of my spiritual father's words. They feed me with guidance and balance me with joy.

Ease is not easiness. I give thanks for the way my spiritual father's counsel gives ease even as the journey remains difficult. Help does not hinder. Help does not solve. Help helps me through and never escapes me out.

Amen.

■ ■ ■

JUNE 15

God, Place of My Falling:

I fall into your grace and find myself upheld.

Your living Word nurses my equilibrium in a topsy-turvy world.

Though I can't see pressure, it is an unforgiving force.

And your grace and wisdom balance the equation, turning pressures into possibilities.

Amen.

■ ■ ■

JUNE 16

God, Most Merciful:

It is as if a cool shower of mercy falls upon my overwhelmed life. Busy. Full. Noisy.

Mercy falls upon me and washes away the husk of doing.

And I feel the open stretch of being calling me to roam unseen fields of worship.

Amen.

■ ■ ■

JUNE 17

God, Mercy Unending:

It is as if mercy is a friend attending to my body in a time of sickness.

I awaken, and mercy is there beside me.

Mercy is the cool glass of water in the heat.

Mercy is the open window to the summer morning breeze.

Mercy is the hum of the honeybees pollinating.

Amen.

JUNE 18

God, Mercy of all Creation:

It is as if mercy is the evening star, first to light the night after sun's retiring.

Strong to say darkness will not undo you.

Mercy lights the way when all else fails.

I will not be left alone to despair in the darkness or the unseeing.

I will look up and feel the ministry of heaven's light tune my heart to the choir of alleluias charting faith's way through the dark night.

Amen.

■ ■ ■

JUNE 19

God for All through Every Season of Life:

It is as if mercy takes my hand through the storm and walks with me to the shelter of silence.

Peace attends me there, and mercy keeps company with the cloud of witnesses before and around me.

Mercy sings to me a song of remembrance. I am not alone, and I gently join in the tune. I am sung by an everlasting light—the hymns of mercy.

Amen.

■ ■ ■

JUNE 20

God, Empire of Tender Mercy for All Who Flee the Rulers of This Age:

It is as if mercy speaks to me words of beauty. They rise amidst the run-down places; the broken places; the ugly scars of civilization gone astray.

Mercy is goodness. Mercy is truth. Mercy is beautiful. Mercy is the ministry of hope that nears just around the corner of faith.

I am astounded to see that even after destruction and despair, mercy's tender flower blooms through the ashes of our tears, up from the darkness of our scars.

Amen.

■ ■ ■

JUNE 21

Son of God, Christ the Light:

The community of living things lives in your light. Everything is eating stored sunlight.

I have lived on sunlight, oxygen, and water. Everything I have eaten also lives on the light. Leafy greens, cows, chickens, fish, grains, grasses, plants, vegetables, all such living things ate the light and grew. Your bread of life is stored light. Your light is the stored energy of eros love. The desire to be and become, overflowing upon this planet from nine light minutes above.

I have fed upon the earth for fifty years. I live by sunlight. I live by oxygen. I live by water.

Amen.

■ ■ ■

JUNE 22

God of Faith's Journey:

Your love shades my journey. I walk into the twilight of being, placing my fears into the strength I can't see.

Your light casts a shadow over the empires of time, marking their limits.

You eclipse us all. And our unknowing is all we really know.

Amen.

■ ■ ■

JUNE 23

Liberating Love of Heaven:

Take my darkness and walk with me into the morning shade.

Awaken me gently with the shock of grace that is the light of Christ's enduring Eucharistic presence, in loving action, silence, prayer, word, and sacrament.

Amen.

■ ■ ■

JUNE 24

Beloved Source of Life:

Take my moody despair and replace it with the joy of arising into the new day of your love, conveyed one breath at a time.

Help me feel my heartbeat of life, and remember I am being lived by life. This gifting is my joy, and this remembrance my awakening.

Amen.

■ ■ ■

JUNE 25

Spirit of the Lord, Who Journeys with Me:

Each turn of season, each decade of life, each year, each week, each day, each hour—your silence overwatches me as a presence of stillness, and I take rest and delight in the clarity that you are my guiding counsel.

Amen.

■ ■ ■

JUNE 26

God, Revealing Light:

Praise arises in the quietness of the evening hours, at day's ending. So too praise arises in the freshness of the morning hours, at day's beginning. I feel your presence with me like an unseen line cast between the fading light of dusk and the dark purple of twilight. I can't tell where one ends and the other begins. As with your presence, you shade into my life unseen yet undeniably definitive.

Amen.

■ ■ ■

JUNE 27

God, Breather of First Life:

Waves of life stream toward the future, with every conception, with every birth. Bless the human family in our growth upon the earth. Bless us with qualities of compassion. Bless us with tenderness toward each other. Teach us the ways of gentleness and cooperation in all our growth and expansion.

Amen.

JUNE 28

Lord Jesus:

Take my hope and cast it toward the everlasting strong center that holds amidst life's fraying.

Let hope catch the light and soar into the strength of Thy gale-force grace.

I am soaring, yet grounded. I am uplifted yet rooted. I stretch forth into this attraction, and I find myself infused with your love drawing new ideas and possibilities, birthing miracles out of the hopeless shards of the past.

Amen.

■ ■ ■

JUNE 29

Creator of the Heavens and Earth:

You are the living sphere of holy love, ever expanding.

I am born and live and have my being within your sphere of life.

So too, everyone and everything.

This perspective changes all my seeing.

And I humbly consent to explore the mystery more and more.

Amen.

■ ■ ■

JUNE 30

O God, Listening Presence:

The hallowed edge of light peels away falseness from my ways of being. Your light shows me false places and the cheap string I've tied my life together with. I see that it barely holds.

So, I often feel life unraveling me from the inside out. I sit in the silence and trust your weaving love will knit my tenderness into strength, my loneliness into community, and my fears into courage.

I know that the word "help" is a simple word, but it is all I really can say right now. And your hearing and listening presence changes everything.

Amen.

JULY

It is as if God says:

Take rest and know that I am God.

Take hope and be at peace.

Take strength and experience that you can do all through Christ.

JULY 1

God of Grace and New Beginnings:

Your Word opens the locked places of my heart.

And I breathe the air of forgiveness.

And I feel the cascading uplift of grace.

Amen.

JULY 2

God of Flourishing Beauty:

I see the golden-hued fields of sunflowers, turning through the day to the light, and I am reminded of the obedience of devotion.

I hear the summer songbirds greet the day and sing their hymns, and I am reminded of the simplicity of worship.

Teach me your ways through the way of beauty and life flourishing in the extraordinary ordinary of earth's seasons.

Amen.

JULY 3

God of the Calling:

I choose to turn my gaze upon your promises, and not be so distracted by life's problems.

I choose to listen for your Word, instead of thinking I have all the answers.

I choose to be among the chosen, instead of drifting in circles in a sea of doubt.

Amen.

■ ■ ■

JULY 4

God, Majesty of All Time and Eternity:

Uphold me in the sky of freedom.

I wish to soar with a seeing eye of faith; to glide on the thermals of devotion, at ease—rejoicing among the community of believers rooted deeply in silent clouds of prayer.

Amen.

JULY 5

Christ, Light of My Life:

You cover me with morning's new light and awaken me gently to see the patterns and choices of my life that need healing and forgiveness.

I weep the tears of repentance and kneel the surrender of confession.

Years and perhaps decades past arise to memory, and I see the mixed person I've been—a contradiction to myself—so faithful and yet also so selfish.

Under the covering of your loving-kindness, past burdens and dissonance are dissolved and resolved forever.

Amen.

■ ■ ■

JULY 6

Guiding Angels of the Lord:

Take my hand and lead me through this phase of the journey.

I am here now, and you are calling me to journey forward in faith. Behind me, nearly everything I know and hold dear.

Ahead, only the unknown and what I feel to be trusted promises—unseen yet utterly compelling.

Help me walk in faith and not look back, second-guessing.

Amen.

■ ■ ■

JULY 7

Ever-Faithful Beloved:

There is a promise that seals my heart.

Your promise fastens to me with tender strength, an unrelenting, kind fervor.

My faith is fueled with its inward mark, deep within, a will to flourish.

Amen.

■ ■ ■

JULY 8

Living Truth, Guiding Love:

Help me understand that love alone fulfills my destiny. And wisdom completes all my inquiries, even if the questions can't be answered.

You are the answer that remains even when I keep my distance, preferring to play with speculation instead of being wed to the knowing beyond knowing.

Amen.

■ ■ ■

JULY 9

Christ, Light-Center Holding Us Together:

When I feel that there is no safe place on this planet, no refuge from others' desires and demands gone astray;

When I feel that I've gone over the edge of the world's care and kindness, sanity and benevolence;

In all such alarms, help me fulfill my destiny to remain in you.

Amen.

JULY 10

God, My Safe Harbor:

When the pain of failure and defeat occurs, lift my mind to remember that holy is the way of unknowing and holy the gift of unseeing. All things are washed in the river of forgetfulness. Everything can rise anew in the sea of forgiveness.

Every seeming vastness has a shore on which to rest, and a cove in which to rebuild.

In your strength, I will sail again.

Amen.

■ ■ ■

JULY 11

Holy God:

I am held by a wind so graceful it lets me bend and bow and yet not break.

I am swayed in these winds—swayed into wonder and praise.

Amen.

JULY 12

Lord Jesus, Living Christ:

I hear you say to the weary, *come to me and I will give you rest.*

I hear you say to the convicted, *your sins are forgiven, go and sin no more.*

I hear you say to the bereaved, *I will never leave you or forsake you.*

Your words live in me, feeding an ancient hunger, nourishing a bone-deep ache.

Amen.

■ ■ ■

JULY 13

Guiding Paraclete through the Decades:

Life is full of paradoxes, and faith is full of ways forward:

Through unknowing, I begin to understand.

Through unseeing, I begin to see.

Though born decades ago, I begin to live.

Amen.

■ ■ ■

JULY 14

Jesus, Healer of Siloam and Bethesda:

There is a darkness in my darkness,

Still, silent, like a cavern's glassy pond.

It feels lifeless. But even your Spirit hovers over the deep and calls it to become.

Even your light permeates this hidden mind-space and speaks words of possibility to the dark in my darkness.

Amen.

■ ■ ■

JULY 15

My God of the Forested Garden:

I walk upon a world of roots, long-lived before I was here and long enduring after I shall pass.

They hold the forest together, intertwined in living nourishment, communication, and love.

I am their student. I am their devotee.

This forest ministers to me. When I can't read or hear another truth, I walk in the silent company of this forested community and remember something I keep forgetting.

Amen.

▦ ▦ ▦

JULY 16

Heavenly God, Birther of Earth's Beginnings:

In a moment of prayer, I see morning dew, still and silent upon the eye-high prairie grass.

I peer into the dew and see a miniature universe, filled with the movement of microscopic life.

The water beads are like jewels glistening in the sunrise. They cling with ease to the swaying grass, dancing in morning's bright breeze.

I remember something about myself standing beside this universe. I remember something about you, my God, source of all life. Everything comes from your first speaking.

Such prairie mornings help me listen.

Amen.

■ ■ ■

JULY 17

Glorious Abba beyond Description:

My body rises with the dawn to praise you.

This frame is not just a casket of desires. My body is a temple of devotion.

A receptor to your Spirit.

A river cascading through this lifetime—following its path to the great sea that is just a drop of your unbounded edge.

Amen.

JULY 18

Christ of the Cloud of Witnesses:

Eucharist, red breath of my life.

Scriptures, black ore of my being.

Song and chant, golden light of my soul.

You are beloved inward friends, guiding me through the crowded dynamics of community life.

Amen.

■ ■ ■

JULY 19

Living God, Giver of This Day:

You are the architect of nature and the author of our arising.

In your wisdom, I find myself.

In your patterns, I see myself and discover my relatedness with others.

In your love, I feel the pulse of my life, in rhythm with all things living.

I kneel in wonder and rise in praise.

I feel that life is an astounding journey, and I thank you for the opportunity to flourish for your glory.

Amen.

■ ■ ■

JULY 20

God, Ground of My Life:

Infuse me with a living faith that knows even as it inquires; a wisdom that teaches even as it learns.

I ponder your Word and discover your ways among and for us.

My mind kneels in wonder, humbled by the darkness of my blindness in the face of your Word's blazing, revelatory light.

In your light I see light.

Amen.

■ ■ ■

JULY 21

Word of God before All Words and Worlds:

In silence and stillness calming words arise in my heart.

These calming words walk with me through conflicted times.

These words bring peace because they are in some measure growing in the grace of your first Word, even if your Word is encircled in silence.

Amen.

■ ■ ■

JULY 22

Life-Changing Presence:

Your presence in and by the Spirit touches me though the stillness of my body, at rest, sitting beside the forest. I hear the wind through the trees, and the strength of its gentle forces ensures me that no matter how much my life might feel in jeopardy by situations, events, or relationships, you meet me in grace and infuse me with a hidden strength. Even if nothing external changes, I discover that by your grace, I have changed—and that makes all the difference.

Amen.

JULY 23

Lord Jesus, Humble Servant to the Power of the Father's Love:

Show me the way of this kind of love: as you have loved the father and as the father loves you.

I see that your strength is powerful in weakness, and that your weakness is a chosen act of love.

I see that your love breaks the laws of man's ideas of power and creates new ways of victory.

And so may I—

    Live in the raiment of your humility;

    Flourish in the arc of your gentle power;

    Thrive in the weak force of your impossible cross—

And yet you turned that too into the possibility of love and forgiveness.

Amen.

JULY 24

Lord Jesus:

Let me not awaken too late, too often, that I miss the grace of your Word speaking to my heart in the morning silence or the evening stillness.

Daily, hourly, moment by moment, I seem to be tossed inwardly between listening and forgetting, awakening and sleeping.

I wish my heart to be more affixed by absorption to and in your leading Word.

Amen.

■ ■ ■

JULY 25

God of All Times, Beyond All Time:

Let me not drift around in the sea of time.

Nor lose my way in the fog of confusion and choices.

Let me take the two hands of time, past and future, and stand in the embrace of time's present body, awake, attuned, activated to choose wisely and engage each moment consciously, gratefully, with the praise of one who understands life's journey is time-bound, and whose given days are unknown and also unrepeatable. Let me cherish each breath of time and become time's student and wise wayfarer.

Amen.

■ ■ ■

JULY 26

O Thou Living God Who Says Let There Be:

I close my eyes, and a screen of memories arises.

I see how I have been. I see who I am becoming.

Then there is a stillness and quiet within. A kind darkness. A gentle expanse.

All stories are washed in the light. Set free, their sentences unbound, they return to the Word, and to silence before the Word.

Amen.

Christ of the Middle Cross:

Holy the desire that sets my sights to creativity.

Holy the difficulty that seems to get in the way.

Holy the sunrise that breaks the difference between night and day.

Amen.

■ ■ ■

JULY 28

Living God Worthy of Praise:

Let praise be spoken through my words today.

Let praise be written through my actions today.

Let praise be seen through my affect and gestures today.

Let praise be felt in the atmosphere I bring into each space I enter today.

Let praise be the breath that animates my living being today.

Amen.

JULY 29

Word of Life:

In the silence of wonder and the stillness of adoration I rediscover that—

You are the under and the over. You are the in and out.

You are the here and beyond. You are the without and within.

You are the around and the about.

You are my everything, even though I never see or hear you with my senses.

You are the mystery that keeps me seeking and the revelation that keeps me kneeling.

Amen.

■ ■ ■

JULY 30

Lord of My Lineage and Lifetime:

The end of July reminds me of many summers in childhood spent at my grandmother and grandfather's pool. Grandpa built it himself, and he loved to begin summer days at 5:00 a.m. alone in the water. Now, decades later, I do the same. I remember as I float on my back, reading the low morning clouds; I remember that I too will slip beyond this world like Grandpa, who died too young of a sudden stroke. I remember the taste of saltines and Sprite after an afternoon of swimming, playing with Grandpa in the pool. His cannonball splashes were unbeatable. I remember the brilliant orange tiger lilies aglow all around the pool's backyard fence. And the sound of the June bugs' lazy buzz. I remember and I am grateful.

Amen.

■ ■ ■

JULY 31

Mother Mary, Care of God:

Tender are the humble ones who let their tears teach the way of love.

Tender are the gracious ones who let their loving touch show the way of love.

Tender are the wise ones who set their words alight with warmth, a life-guiding-light.

Tender are the hearts of your brothers and sisters in the family of your Son.

Amen.

AUGUST

It is as if I join the summer clouds, aloft in praise yet grounded in song, hymning:

> O Joy I have not fully known.
> O Jesus, splendid upon Thy throne.
> Enter now we, the gates of glory.
> Eternal City, Jerusalem,
> In us complete Thy Godward story.

AUGUST 1

Holy Ground of All Creation:

It may be that we are to be humbled, so to live more attentively to your sustaining power.

For Earth does not know how many times it has turned.

Nor Sun remember the year or decade, according to our culturally agreed-upon calendar.

Names of days and months and the year's number are structures human mind has placed upon our experience of being here on Earth as it rotates daily and circles annually around our great sun.

So, teach me to number my days and live accordingly, reverently, humbly.

Amen.

■ ■ ■

AUGUST 2

Beloved Word of Earth's Foundation:

Yes, always, and forever, your grace turns every page into a new chapter.

And yet when I see the wasteland desert, and the dead burning tree,

And the heated, lifeless sea, a bitter sorrow arises in my mouth, and warm tears fall, heavily. I see how the human family has lived upon the earth and now it seems the toll is too high to pay.

Have mercy upon us. I don't know how a new story can arise without a burning of the book of old ways.

Amen.

■ ■ ■

AUGUST 3

Spirit of Peace:

Where there is strife, bring love. Open the closed circuits of resistance and transform every locked circle into a spiral of new possibility.

Your presence changes everything.

Amen.

■ ■ ■

AUGUST 4

Spirit of Truth and Wisdom:

Guided by the stars of your leading lights, St. John Chapter 14 shows me the way and Ephesians Chapter 3 teaches me how to pray. Though it may seem easier to take this journey moment by moment, a kind of simple dead reckoning, turn by turn, gives me a heart orientated to your love, grace, and truth. I start with listening to the Scripture in silence—and, like a shadowed grace, an internal mental map arises, and your truths match the longings of my soul's journey.

Amen.

■ ■ ■

AUGUST 5

O God:

Disturb me until I love Thee.

Turn my ambivalence into abiding.

Amen.

■ ■ ■

AUGUST 6

God of Jubilation:

You spoke the universe into form.

You redeemed it out of chaos.

Fill me with a new song of praise and thanksgiving.

Invigorate my being with your love.

Amen.

■ ■ ■

AUGUST 7

O God of My Entirety:

Your strong voice fills my heart with quiet words.

Your Scripture fills my mind with silence.

Your wisdom fills my being with directed attention.

Amen.

■ ■ ■

AUGUST 8

Christ Jesus:

You are Lord of the Way—the Way of flame and rose; cross and glory; fire and wind; spark and light.

The indulgence of life abounds all around, and your fecundity toward us is a fierce mercy.

Again and again, you calm the storms of our making with the quiet imprint of your beholding.

Amen.

■ ■ ■

AUGUST 9

O Eternal Descent of Love:

May your flaming fire of wisdom enlighten, guide, and heal.

May texts of divinity enliven understanding and justice.

May the Word of God birth simple humility in more of us.

Amen.

AUGUST 10

O Eternal Arising of Love:

May the passion of the sons and daughters of Abraham leave its mark of hope deep within the afflicted and lead us anew into the holiness of the present moment, even amidst our shards of affliction. And may we return homeward together.

Amen.

■ ■ ■

AUGUST 11

Beloved of My Being:

You are my deepest breath and my strongest heartbeat.

You are the light of my mind and the strength of my body.

You are my life, hope, and everything.

In you I live, move, and have my being.

Amen.

■ ■ ■

AUGUST 12

O Lord Our God:

You—

Speak in silence.

Teach my ignorance.

Heal my sickness.

Mend my brokenness.

Comfort my mourning.

Strengthen my weakness.

Forgive my aimlessness.

Remove my guilt and shame.

Transform my will.

Set me free from sin.

Raise me to a new life.

Amen.

AUGUST 13

O Lord My God:

I also look to the other.

To know that I am not alone on this journey.

To gain hope by the other's example.

To gain strength from the other's fellowship.

To enjoy a shoulder to lean on when weary.

To receive a hug when lonely.

And wise words when I don't know the way.

Amen.

■ ■ ■

AUGUST 14

O God:

Behold my inner being.

Behold my inmost self.

Behold my searching mind.

Behold the affections of my heart.

Behold my way.

Behold my direction.

Behold my being and accompany me through the mystery of my coming and going.

Amen.

■ ■ ■

AUGUST 15

God of All:

I am for peace, yet when I speak it seems others are for war.

Let my words not agitate. Let my words not distress.

Enfold my language in the peace of love and the honey of wisdom.

Amen.

AUGUST 16

God for All:

Too much, the world is, for me. But not for you.

Remind me today how much you are for everyone, everywhere.

How much your love grows toward the edge of light, where the darkness starts, and miracles begin.

Amen.

■ ■ ■

AUGUST 17

God with All:

When feeling alone, abandoned or forsaken, I am reminded of your connecting presence, no matter where I am. Your love, your remembrance, your great regard are with me, with anyone, anywhere.

I am accompanied, and though circumstances may look dire, your absence instructs me there is something more than this world.

Amen.

AUGUST 18

God toward All in Christ:

I feel your risen presence as the very life that pervades and yet transcends my body and my mind. I realize you are the Way and the Truth, and I am grateful to share in your life turned toward me, toward all.

Amen.

■ ■ ■

AUGUST 19

God of the Scriptures:

I take the inward turn today, to hear and remember the truths of your Way.

Your Word has called and formed many through the generations—and in that pairing a bond of love is formed that fuels a faith that can endure trials and difficulties with inward peace.

Inwardly, may your Word land in a soft place, take root, and feed me the living tradition of the Apostles and the founding grace of Christ.

Amen.

AUGUST 20

Abba, Foundation of My Life:

I am listening in the stillness.

I am quiet. Consented. Collected unto the silence.

I am, because you are, have always been, and will always be.

Amen.

■ ■ ■

AUGUST 21

Peaceful Presence after the Storm:

The quiet of stillness is my strength.

As I attend to this quiet, your Word draws me downward into the depths of surrender and the heights of freedom from desire.

Amen.

■ ■ ■

AUGUST 22

Light of the World:

I am a particle in the expression of your love.

Your expression of yourself reaches into me as the source of my life, all life, and colors my being *as an expressed one*.

We are the family of expressed ones. Expressions of your creative energy. Expressions of your choice to be for us beyond our ability to be for ourselves. Our family name is imprinted with the same desire of the Desirer who started the journey with the first expression: *Let there be*.

Amen.

■ ■ ■

AUGUST 23

Self-Existent One, Source of All Creation:

The universe is your gesture of benevolence toward us, a secure reality of form, undeniable to the senses and inspiring to the soul. The force of beauty lifts us up from despair. The scale of grandeur appropriates our forlornness and transforms it into worship.

That there is anything and not nothing is your validity and our security.

Amen.

■ ■ ■

AUGUST 24

Humble Lord of Gethsemane:

Open my awareness to watch with you in the garden of our world, to listen for the suffering of God as well as the cries of the suffering.

I wish to live unreservedly abandoned unto the way of unknowing: to the listening way, to the silent tears of prayer, to night's betrayal of the light, and the strong action of rising to face the powers of opposition with consent into your powerful weakness.

Amen.

■ ■ ■

AUGUST 25

Accompanying Presence:

Continue your overshadowing care upon my journey, even as it turns into uncharted shadows.

You are the light of love imprinting my heart, anointing me with consolations through Scripture and silence.

Amen.

■ ■ ■

AUGUST 26

Leader through Life's Labyrinths:

I survey past choices of years gone by.

I peer into the future of new days to come.

I am not lost. I am found in you. Even as I can't see the next step, I know you are with me, leading through the turns, always moving toward the center, even if it feels like the edge of nowhere.

Amen.

AUGUST 27

All-seeing Spirit of God:

Your presence touches my inward awareness, helping me see myself as I have been, with total clarity.

I see your patience has journeyed beside my inconsistency and betrayals, ever waiting for my awakening to see the shallowness with which I have loved you.

Tears of conviction cleanse my seeing and being, and fed by this sorrow of heart, I begin again, forgiven, restored, released from the chains of my unfaithfulness.

Amen.

■ ■ ■

AUGUST 28

Beloved Redeemer:

I do not fear the work of your grace, even as it cuts into the softness of my memory and the hardness of my heart.

I see now how I have preferred my own words to your Word, and my own spiritual comforts to the consolation of your cross.

Amen.

AUGUST 29

Lord Jesus of the Father's Love:

In the cold corners of my will, the hiddenness of your Word warms my way despite my selfish choices and forgetfulness of past mercies.

I kneel in the cathedral of my lifetime and bow out of the game I've played to be in charge.

Your love defeats me. The victory of your Word heals me. I am yours.

Amen.

■ ■ ■

AUGUST 30

Lord Jesus, Regent of Everlasting Life:

I hear your Word. It is sounding forth in a very deep, rare, and tender place. Its tenderness is open to your mending.

Your Word rules with gentleness, and your power guides with peace.

I consent and choose your choice for me.

Amen.

AUGUST 31

Lord Jesus, Prince of the Way of Humility:

The games played to win in this world are empty castles built on clouds.

Dominant culture reveals its roots are grounded in corruption.

Life apart from your presence is untenable.

Little here brings joy.

I need your saving. I need your help.

Amen.

SEPTEMBER

Returning, there are rhythms woven into our bodies.

Schoolroom. Playground. School bus. Lunch box.

After school practice.

Football season.

Cooler nights.

The earth is preparing us for changes.

Year by year, families grow and learn.

Year by year, life takes us forward.

SEPTEMBER 1

Heart-rending Word of Grace:

Life stretches the sinews of my faith. The lies of leaders. The corruption of the system. The despair of the downtrodden. This all cracks my hope and tears my joy into dust.

Where this pains the most, enter the tender places with your promises that cover the face of the dark chaos with righteous new beginnings.

Amen.

■ ■ ■

SEPTEMBER 2

Beloved Master of the Gospel:

Your Word pairs with my affections, and a sweetness ripens in this union.

I feel your living presence of love, named among the saints and centuries of devotion.

I am living flame too, alight by the stream of light radiating from the first anointed ones of Pentecost and the first listening ones of Galilee.

You are with me even now, long centuries later. And I am
with you.

Amen.

■ ■ ■

SEPTEMBER 3

Holy Trinity of Encircling Love:

I hear your prompting in the silence.

I feel your presence in the stillness.

It is not all of you, but even just this faraway echo is
unmistakably holy and overwhelmingly beautiful.

I kneel in the atmosphere of wonder and awe.

I sing with upstretched arms in the spirit of surrender.

We come to life in your far-casting shadow.

Amen.

■ ■ ■

SEPTEMBER 4

God, Creator:

Gently, the light falls upon us through the eyes of another.

In each other, we see your first light.

I praise you, source of all letting be.

Amen.

■ ■ ■

SEPTEMBER 5

God of My Salvation:

Folded into the filaments of my desire, I see a golden thread.

I name this seam loving-kindness and feel the garment of your grace enfolding my lifetime.

Amen.

■ ■ ■

SEPTEMBER 6

Christ Jesus the Way:

Guide my first step of faith into the horizon before me.

Guide my last step of sorrow through the edge of despair.

Guide my middle steps of perseverance along the narrow path of obedience.

Amen.

■ ■ ■

SEPTEMBER 7

God of the Covenants:

Gentle light of the morning, you shape my listening and form my knowing.

Early Eden lingers like a long-cast shadow, in the morning stillness.

I remember something beyond what words can say, and I lift my heart in praise,

Remembering I am of the family of the redeemed.

Amen.

SEPTEMBER 8

Creator God of the I Am:

I see how many strive to make their name in the world.

The power to name, and the glory of being named.

Author. Owner. Builder. Names on books. Names on office doors. Names on the tops of buildings and the tails of planes. Names on funds. Names on patents. Names on schools and hospitals and streets.

Names on nations, states, rivers, seas, and continents. Even names on stars and sister galaxies.

Wherever we go, we name. Like our creator, we name.

But wherever our name might be or not be, what matters most is that we are named:

That we are named the beloved, the son, the daughter, a secret name appointed for our inward heart, by you, the I Am beyond all names.

Amen.

■ ■ ■

SEPTEMBER 9

Lord, Savior:

Save me with your peace from my inclination to fear.

Sometimes it seems every cell in my body is laden with fear's sinking feeling, and my mind sees only despair.

You are Lord because you save me, and you save me because you are Lord.

Amen.

■ ■ ■

SEPTEMBER 10

Faithful Presence:

Your Word shadows the life-parched places of my soul, giving ease.

Your Word is like the presence of water in the desert— changing everything.

Amen.

■ ■ ■

SEPTEMBER 11

Faithful Love:

I praise you, God of faithful love, for you have drawn the universe into being, and its silent presence colors the darkness with an eternal chorus of lights.

Your faithful love is a fountain of desire, and all becoming flows from your open center, bearing everything into being.

Amen.

■ ■ ■

SEPTEMBER 12

Leading Gentle Light:

Daily, your light lifts me up into a new discovery of myself— and I see that the old lines drawn by hardships have woven a map of your mercy over the face of my lifetime.

Amen.

■ ■ ■

SEPTEMBER 13

Ever-Faithful God:

The inward place of depth, this ancient pool of stillness gathers within my kneeling.

So too the tender touch of your Word follows every step I take.

Still or walking, you rove with me on this lifetime journey—and I know the joy of your faithfulness.

Amen.

■ ■ ■

SEPTEMBER 14

Holy Spirit, Reconciling Presence:

I look to your Word today.

Shape my understanding when teachings confuse.

Ease my frustrations when life resists my dreams and choices.

Cool my anger when friction ignites.

And expand my view when misunderstandings clog up joyful relating.

Amen.

■ ■ ■

SEPTEMBER 15

Holy Spirit, Holy Presence:

Your quiet way of leading is a silence for the tenderhearted.

And a song for the humbled.

I am listening.

I am singing.

I can be a nave for your silence.

Amen.

■ ■ ■

SEPTEMBER 16

Jesus, Lord of the Way:

Expand my empathy beyond the blind spots of my personality.

Guide my understanding through curvy roads of knowledge.

Bless my will as I make choices at every turn of life.

I know you can turn every dead end into a flourishing new beginning.

Amen.

■ ■ ■

SEPTEMBER 17

Holy God of the Shekinah Light:

Your breath of life is my arising.

The mark of your name upon my heart never blurs or shades.

The harmony of your Word within my mind never mutes or fades.

I rejoice today in this unbroken fellowship that weaves all that is me with an infinitesimal part of your glory.

Amen.

■ ■ ■

SEPTEMBER 18

Ever-Faithful Light of the World:

Day by day, I am shaped by your mercies, held by your grace, enfolded by your wisdom, and sent forth by your strength.

Amen.

■ ■ ■

SEPTEMBER 19

God, Source of Peace:

Infuse my nervous system with the healing calm of your presence. I feel swamped by emotions of frustration and anger. So much seems to be going in the wrong direction, and I feel that I have no control or ability to change it.

Touch the water of this situation and turn it into the new wine, replacing aggravation with joy.

Amen.

■ ■ ■

SEPTEMBER 20

Abba of the Risen Lord:

Teach me to understand more deeply the words of Christ Jesus.

Teach me to share more fully the message of Christ Jesus.

Teach me to embody the love of Christ Jesus.

Amen.

■ ■ ■

SEPTEMBER 21

Faithful and Forgiving Pilot of My Life:

I see the ways I have gone astray, pursuing ideas or theories that promised more than they could deliver.

Why have I been so embarrassed by your Gospel? Why so timid to embrace your truth? Why so willing to chase esoteric ideas that only filter the radiance of your grace and revelation?

Nevertheless, I praise you, O Lord, for in your silent way, you steered my journey through it all back to you and the simplicity of faith and devotion to Jesus, Lord Savior.

Amen.

■ ■ ■

SEPTEMBER 22

Lord Jesus Christ the Betrayed:

Teach me not to react or seek revenge. Lead me in the way of peace into the freedom of being so grounded in the truth of your love that even the worst slander or misrepresentation takes no hold in the soil of my being—because it is not truth.

Amen.

■ ■ ■

SEPTEMBER 23

Beloved of My Lifetime:

Your love measures my life with broad mercy.

Your love draws my life out into new possibilities.

Your love anoints my life with many sunrises of new beginnings and sunsets of benediction.

Beginning or ending, I am at peace, for you are with me.

Amen.

■ ■ ■

SEPTEMBER 24

God, Who Journeys by Stages with Me:

Edges emerge in every calling and vocation, phases in every job and career.

Sometimes there is an abrupt ending. Sometimes just an unexpected turn. And sometimes everything is overturned.

If this is the end of my role, give me the courage to be faithful without scorn.

Give me the assurance that you walk with me into the unknown, toward a new endeavor more suited to my gifts, skills, and dreams.

Amen.

■ ■ ■

SEPTEMBER 25

Holy Lord of Lords:

Your kingdom is a gentle power, yet a fierce force of love.

Shape my mind with your reigning truth.

Your reign is a revealing and healing light, a noncontentious power grounded in your choice to be an open space for all to be born into the fullness of what can be.

Shape my life in congruence with your vulnerable dominion, in harmony with the agency of your ever-faithful mercies.

Amen.

■ ■ ■

SEPTEMBER 26

Jesus Christ, Our Yes to Life:

I trust the victory of your love.

I trust the victory of your love even through the dark nights where fear and loneliness play recklessly in the fields of my imagination.

I trust the victory of your love.

Amen.

■ ■ ■

SEPTEMBER 27

Lord Jesus of the Cross:

The weight of life presses me down into low places where only hope breathes.

My heart is porous, receiving whatever gifts this barren space might give.

And your Word lives to speak again, raising every fraction of my self into the new being you promised when you once said on a dark afternoon at Golgotha to a fellow pilgrim of the fellowship of the porous heart: *today you will be with me in paradise.*

Amen.

■ ■ ■

SEPTEMBER 28

Lord God, Creator of the Heavens and the Earth:

Hand upon my head, I feel the warmth of your wisdom alighting upon me.

Hand upon my heart, I feel your tempo keeping watch over my lifetime.

Hand upon my belly, I feel your gentle force of life breathing me.

And I praise Thee, Lord, for the gift of being a part of your world of worlds.

Amen.

■ ■ ■

SEPTEMBER 29

God of Perfect Timing:

Transform my waiting into awaiting.

Move the mountains that seem to block my journey.

And open the doors of time that seem stuck in the past or present. Bring about the new.

I am awaiting your move, Lord. I will follow.

Amen.

■ ■ ■

SEPTEMBER 30

God of Every Season:

Your cadence of light moves with silent rhythms into and through the substance of all things.

Alight within, we are each a vessel of your presence.

You journey with us, even unseen.

Passages of days, weeks, and months turn into seasons, then years.

Decades peel away. Time melts into the sea.

And our breath returns to your first embrace.

Amen.

OCTOBER

It is as if God says:

Change comes slowly, and sometimes suddenly.

I am the amber light and the golden wisdom.

I am the certain thunder far away, coming to you.

My glory shakes the earth. My power drenches the earth with rain.

My presence makes everything flourish.

I am the loving communion holding all things together, even as alternative forces take their moment in the sun to work their magic, only to see it all undone.

OCTOBER 1

God before the Beginning:

Amidst the cold mind of culture, I feel a kindled affection for the Scriptures.

Your wisdom draws me into the warmth of worship.

As I lift my heart in praise, I discover that your Word is the awakening balm to all that numbs and keeps me asleep to the wonders of your works among and for us.

Amen.

■ ■ ■

OCTOBER 2

Lord Jesus, Healing Name and Presence:

Touch the empty places in my life with your grace.

And touch the sorrowful spaces with your joy.

Amen.

OCTOBER 3

Holy Spirit:

Your love enters the closed parts of my heart.

There, your presence changes everything, like morning fog lifting in a valley.

I feel joy again. And I see clearly. I am not alone.

Amen.

■ ■ ■

OCTOBER 4

Jesus, Prince of Peace:

Suddenly, the dark edge of worry cuts into my peace.

And anxiety is a jagged guest, arriving without warning.

Help me remember to yawn, laugh, and rub my belly—to awaken my body as an ark of safety from the storms of trauma.

And I will speak your name of peace, again and again, in my heart with sound and silence, knowing everything distressful about my life can be forgotten by remembering your name.

Amen.

■ ■ ■

OCTOBER 5

Lord Jesus Christ the Risen One:

I trust you. I love you. I know that every night of loss will end with the dawn of an unexpected new beginning.

Embraced by that first Sunday morning Jerusalem joy, I grow in the light of your resurrection.

Amen.

■ ■ ■

OCTOBER 6

God of Transformation:

Refine everything in me that is usable for your glory and the embodiment of your Word.

Remove everything in me that is unusable, unyielding, and opposed to your love.

Amen.

■ ■ ■

OCTOBER 7

God, My Redeemer:

I kneel my words before your Word.

I bow my ideas and thinking before your Wisdom.

I lay down my spiritual sophistication and systems before the clarity, simplicity, and generosity of your Gospel.

Forgive my wanderings into curiosities that only lead to further confusion and keep me from knowing the joy of your saving grace.

Amen.

■ ■ ■

OCTOBER 8

Christ Jesus, Joy of My Salvation:

You are the gentle dawn that lights my life.

You are the bright morning star that dims the night.

You are the high noon truth that covers all with love.

You are the evening quiet that calms all who worry.

You are the dusky hour that puts the weary world to rest.

You are the midnight dark that speaks beyond all words the praises of creation.

Amen.

■ ■ ■

OCTOBER 9

Holy Spirit, Guide for All Truth Seekers:

I delight in your Way.

I adore your Word.

I rejoice in your Wisdom.

You are the breath of my being and the joy of my becoming.

Amer.

■ ■ ■

OCTOBER 10

God of the Seasons:

I enter the kingdom of praise through the gates of October.

Everywhere I look, the earth is consenting to all that the slanting light is doing.

Golden forest.

Crisp morning.

Quiet lane beyond the freshly mown field.

Evening's silent lake, tenderly fading into the starry night.

With these gifts, I am sustained in life and lifted in adoration.

The beauty of this season is also a dying, and it calls to me: *account for your days so to gain a wise heart.*

Amen.

OCTOBER 11

Holy Trinity of the Threefold Gifts:

I praise you this early autumn day; as I reflect upon my life, I see the clear tracks of your presence with me.

A first love—and my new life in Christ began.

A double brokenness—and my mind cracked open beyond doubt into faith.

A triple hope—for the forgiveness of the past, for the grace of the present, and the transformation of the future.

Amen.

■ ■ ■

OCTOBER 12

Author and Perfector of My Life:

Your redemption turns the page on the unworkable storyline of my personality and begins a new chapter of the regeneration of my being.

In Christ, I remember and discover I am a new creation.

By your Spirit, a new name arises within my heart, and you write a new story for a yet to be written book of my journey in your larger, ever-unfolding book of life.

Amen.

■ ■ ■

OCTOBER 13

God of Liberation and Connection:

Your love anoints my life with the charism of joy.

I see how much you help me be more than just me.

Your love is a fusion molding me into a we.

Amen.

■ ■ ■

OCTOBER 14

Holy Spirit, Healing Presence:

Transform my eyes, my words, my actions, my disposition, and my affect into an icon of your healing.

Gather the fragmented pieces of my life into love's encompassing wholeness.

Amen.

■ ■ ■

OCTOBER 15

Living Christ of the Empty Tomb:

I feel your presence in the stillness of the dark before dawn.

I let myself ponder the mystery you are in the silence.

Silence and stillness are your messengers attending to the earth and shaping the empty space our mind fills with words and images.

Amen.

■ ■ ■

OCTOBER 16

Strength of the Gentle Way:

Convey to me—

The tempered power of patience.

The enthroned grandeur of humility.

And the radiant splendor of meekness.

Amen.

■ ■ ■

OCTOBER 17

Jesus, Lord of the Calm:

Hallow the ambivalent space in between my obedience and doubt.

Hallow the distressed face of the one I turn from when I'm too busy to notice their pain.

Hallow the frenzied pace of these overloaded days and help me feel calm amidst the storm.

Amen.

■ ■ ■

OCTOBER 18

Living Word of Life:

The soft breath of ancient words lives within my heart.

These words are still speaking to me within the silence and devotion of my soul's chambers.

Everything that I know to be me now kneels before the open book of Scripture, listening, attending, pondering.

I am not only deeply reading; I am being deeply read.

Amen.

■ ■ ■

OCTOBER 19

Glories of the Heavenly Presence Shining upon Thy Creation:

With the fixity of your light, bend my apprehensions of doubts into convictions of wisdom.

And with the fluidity of your love, shape my animosities of judgment into altruisms of care.

Amen.

OCTOBER 20

God, My Beloved:

Give me the courage to take the path of unnoticed presence in the world.

To turn the corner into obscurity and choose the way of humility.

Amen.

■ ■ ■

OCTOBER 21

Jesus, My Brother in the Night of Prayer:

I'm standing on the edge of the known and safe.

I see that freedom is too powerful—and I am aware how my own choices have the capacity to change nearly everything about my life.

If I choose this new way, what will happen?

I can see how this new choice will upend my comforts and security, even my daily and weekly patterns, my sense of familiarity and control.

I am flooded with "What If?" questions.

But you stand upon the sea of my life and lift me up.

Amen.

■ ■ ■

OCTOBER 22

Jesus, Living Shepherd of My Soul:

You are the peace that feeds my gnawing worries.

You are the strength that lifts my weakness into service.

And you are the name written upon my heart; the name shines into the darkness ahead.

Amen.

■ ■ ■

OCTOBER 23

Jesus of My Life's Journey:

My future is like a beckoning lantern in a forest, far down the trail.

But recently, it seems the lantern has shattered, and all the hope of its light seems to have fallen away into the darkness.

Lord Jesus, be for me a guide brighter than the light and safer than the known.

Amen.

■ ■ ■

OCTOBER 24

God of Overwhelming Understanding:

Numbered concerns await my attention.

Wisdom is needed to navigate each one.

Help me feel what needs to be felt so I may courageously decide what needs to be decided, with comprehensive clarity and wisdom.

Amen.

■ ■ ■

OCTOBER 25

God of the Cloud of Witnesses:

Can I serve without security?

Can I choose the little way of obscurity?

Can I accept the call into the unknown?

Yes, even more, when I feel the calm consent into your faithful love in this quiet space.

Amen.

■ ■ ■

OCTOBER 26

Lord of My Longings:

A holy discontent hovers over the life I am living.

I regret the choices I've made, and I would like to undo them.

I'd like to live elsewhere.

I'd like to be more financially secure so as not to worry and be released to serve others as needs arise.

And most of all, I'd like to be a part of a wise and loving spiritual community, grounded in the Scriptures and sacred worship.

Amen.

■ ■ ■

OCTOBER 27

Holy Presence through All of Creation:

I enter the gates of the glory of autumn praising the colors of life and death, beginnings and endings.

I praise the cool mornings and the brilliant blue northern sky.

Autumn is my teacher, instructing me in the way of release and surrender to the journey of letting go.

Amen.

■ ■ ■

OCTOBER 28

Holy Perfect Divinity:

Your grace is like a liquid light flowing through the complete sphere of my life.

There are no corners or lost turns not drenched in your mercy and high-capacity love.

Amen.

■ ■ ■

OCTOBER 29

Center Point of Grace:

I feel plunged into an upheaval of life that overflows all knowns and floods all familiar pathways and patterns.

In this season of unmooring, be my foundation and center point amidst all the turnings.

Amen.

■ ■ ■

OCTOBER 30

Center Point of Peace:

Cascading voices of motherly tenderness roll through the memories of my lifetime.

Amidst a world bracing itself daily for tumult and raising its fists in tyranny and violence, your voice of blessedness is a center point of healing peace.

Amen.

■ ■ ■

OCTOBER 31

One-Pointed Holy Triune Presence:

A multitude of distractions keeps my attention in motion.

Calm all turbulence into a one-pointed moment of holy remembering: *nothing can separate me from your love.*

Amen.

NOVEMBER

It is as if God says:

I am the ancient presence calling you home.

Gather with your beloveds and feel the strength of love weaving generations together.

Remembering is the seed of gratitude, and joy is the flower of your family heritage.

NOVEMBER 1

Overshadowing Creator Spirit:

Life is a long hello and a slow farewell.

A leaving even amidst the living.

Once born, nothing can stop dying.

Teach me to number and remember my days so to live wisely and joyfully in the shadow of the Lord of this and every moment.

Amen.

■ ■ ■

NOVEMBER 2

Christ Jesus of the Emmaus Road:

A heated intensity of decisions unfolds, undoing years of stability, inviting faith to journey in a new way—wiser now than before. You walk with me in the cool dawn of a new season, and I am not alone.

Amen.

NOVEMBER 3

Reigning Court of Heaven:

I pray that every frayed, failed human leader would turn upward to the wisdom of listening instead of speaking. I pray that your Word becomes a revelation of who I can become when I consent to your love.

Amen.

■ ■ ■

NOVEMBER 4

God through the Storm:

After the tumult, a still, quiet peace.

An ease of breath and being.

Feeling and knowing all is well.

Amen.

■ ■ ■

NOVEMBER 5

God of New Mercies, Morning by Morning:

Let your loving light of guidance dissolve clouds of confusion.

Daylight attends to perplexity, revealing clarity.

The night passes and dawn opens the new day's door, hand in hand with her twin sister, wisdom.

Amen.

■ ■ ■

NOVEMBER 6

God My All in All:

I see how I have placed unreasonable demands and unrealistic expectations on others.

Ease me toward a pleasant release into the peace of contentment and the joy of an uncomplicated simplicity of life.

Amen.

NOVEMBER 7

Christ Jesus, My Way:

In the silence I discover a kind favor, a generous listening.

In the stillness, I enter open spaces with room for discernment, allowing wide turns into ever-new territory.

Amen.

■ ■ ■

NOVEMBER 8

Lord God of Sacred Providence:

Today, I wish to feel the joy and certainty that my recent past is complete.

The liberating assurance that the door is closed and a new one is opening.

Bless this ending with the seal of celebration, and the courage to never look back again in doubt.

Together, we move onward into the warmth of your unfolding invitation to follow.

Amen.

NOVEMBER 9

Holy God before all Beginnings:

I wish to reclaim a sense of your faithfulness.

An awareness of how my lifetime has been kept safe in the cleft of your stillness—even as everything moves fast and ends abruptly.

You are the eternal mother beyond time, the unyielding presence to which I yield.

Amen.

■ ■ ■

NOVEMBER 10

Fire of Heaven:

Your light burns without wounding.

Your fire ignites without scorching.

Your heat consumes without wilting.

I'm listening for the fire burning within every letter of every word the Scriptures enlighten within me.

Amen.

NOVEMBER 11

Rain of Heaven:

Fall upon the dry places of my life.

Bring joy again to the late seasons of fatigue and failure.

Amen.

■ ■ ■

NOVEMBER 12

Christ, Living Water for the Journey:

There is a sweetness I remember.

I return season by season to draw nourishment from your silent Scriptures, ever blessing me with the guidance I need.

Amen.

■ ■ ■

NOVEMBER 13

Lord Jesus, Door to Wider Growth:

I bear witness to change with peace and calm.

As new doors open, and past doors close—I stand in awe of your faithful love through it all.

Amen.

■ ■ ■

NOVEMBER 14

Everlasting Word:

In the silence of remembering, I feel the presence of your rebuke.

Your hard words turn my heart soft—now, I am deeply listening.

Now, I can worship, not just ponder.

Amen.

■ ■ ■

NOVEMBER 15

God of All Peoples:

Heal the fragmented ways I see others.

Help me see beyond the surface of personality, opinions, likes and dislikes, and remember our common wholeness as the endless waves of humanity in the sea of your creativity.

Amen.

■ ■ ■

NOVEMBER 16

Spirit of Wisdom, beyond All Ages and Events:

Teach me how to keep watch in the cave of wisdom, the chamber of devotion.

May this heart-space of mine expand in capacity to learn, remember, and embody, and not only keep faithful vigil on the edges of cultural decay, but also keep advancing peaceful knowledge toward the consummation of the descent of the cloud of understanding.

Amen.

NOVEMBER 17

Holy Comfort of the Burdened and Guardian of the Night:

At the edge of sleep, a restlessness agitates mind and body.

I imagine worst-case scenarios. Anxiety arises.

I breathe deeply, reminding myself that the dark hours of the early morning are not the time to make decisions. This shadow will pass.

Wait for the morning light.

Amen.

■ ■ ■

NOVEMBER 18

Jesus, Way-Maker of Forgiveness:

Shards of slander cut, but not too deep.

Your mercy covers me with gentle tears that sluff off all words lacking truth and love.

And I dwell in your Word, sheltered from the passing storm.

Your Word is a cave of stillness and an anchor of strength.

Amen.

NOVEMBER 19

Christ the Good:

Bequeath to me a joyful disposition as I go through the interactions of this day.

Draft upward into my soul the genius of your inspiration, so that all that is good in me might be useful for all that is challenging for another.

Amen.

■ ■ ■

NOVEMBER 20

Christ the Truth:

Enrich my mind in the firmament of wisdom grounded in the scriptures of history and the understanding still being born in me, and in others.

Lift me into the cloud of faith and place me in just the right calling.

Amen.

■ ■ ■

NOVEMBER 21

Christ the Beautiful:

Imprint my being with the beauty of gentleness and the strength of humility.

Your cross is the beauty of weakness, poured out like a powerful cup of faithfulness upon ever-shattered humanity now gathered into your satiating heart.

Amen.

▪ ▪ ▪

NOVEMBER 22

Christ, Imprint of the Father's Love:

You lift my countenance into the still softness of a new day, buoyed by the joy of freedom.

I feel your belovedness nearing, despite comforts and certainties departing.

Amen.

▪ ▪ ▪

NOVEMBER 23

God, Ever Holy:

Your word consecrates in me an altar of thanksgiving, a vestibule for praise.

I stand with arms up-reaching, and I kneel with head bowed low, feeling the presence of your stillness, like the calm before a storm.

Amen.

■ ■ ■

NOVEMBER 24

God, Ever First Grace:

You reach out to my heart with a part of yourself.

You bind your grace to my life and guide me even when I can't see.

This pairing of your grace to my journey is the anchor point of my life—and I give you thanks!

Amen.

NOVEMBER 25

Lord Jesus, Faithful Shepherd:

Certain of your guiding, and awake to your Spirit's prompting, I humbly walk forward into the unknowns of this day, alert to the subtle intimations your presence provides.

No matter the situation, I am not alone. I am not without resources. I am paired and connected deeply with the deep.

Amen.

■ ■ ■

NOVEMBER 26

God of Glory:

You are close. Your silence speaks to my mind in the stillness.

My breath is quiet and simple. My disposition, at ease.

It is as if my whole life is the first morning of creation.

Amen.

NOVEMBER 27

God of Gravity and Grace:

You are the closeness I feel when all alone.

The warmth attending to my tears after the cold emptiness of being judged, misunderstood, slandered.

Your closeness at the edge of despair is like a blast of arctic air, getting my attention, standing upright, facing forward toward the horizon of new responsibilities.

Amen.

■ ■ ■

NOVEMBER 28

Christ, Regent of the Heart:

Where I feel pressed by time, expand my perception of possibilities.

Where I feel constrained by space, open my vistas of contentment.

You are my all and everything; there is nothing I lack.

Amen.

NOVEMBER 29

Jesus, Worthy One of Adoration:

May your light lance the darkness and weave your wisdom into the fabric of my thinking.

Deepen my capacity to understand.

Expand my willingness to forgive.

Show me your way of being and doing, now and always.

Amen.

■ ■ ■

NOVEMBER 30

Holy Spirit of Refuge:

The cobalt crows fly south, but some stay through the winter.

Black against the early snow, their outlines announce the beauty of contrast and the contours of beauty.

Your life is living in all of us—and I need help loving the contrast of others, especially this Advent.

Transform all the chaos and contrast of our culture into a communion of appreciation and reverence for the different lines we trace back to you, our forever homeland, to which we take flight.

Amen.

DECEMBER

Again, we return to the season of light's darkest hue.

And night's coldest furrows.

Stretched across the dark sky new stars arise.

We feel the wonder of warmth and the presence of beloveds.

Echoes of eternity chant in our hearts.

We wish to give. We wish to care.

Woven together through the celebrations, we perceive
a child rising in each of us.

And we remember something of our holiness.

Something of our beginnings.

Something of our becomings.

DECEMBER 1

Ancient Risen Light:

Anoint this solstice season with a sensitivity to your presence—robing all matter and energy and all human endeavors for the crowning good of planet Earth, this one and the one to come.

Amen.

■ ■ ■

DECEMBER 2

Early Light before the Dawn of Everything:

Christ, Son, you are the light of the world.

Your poignant restfulness is drawing all my weariness into your ease and the sabbath of inner sustenance.

Amen.

■ ■ ■

DECEMBER 3

Light of Life Shining in the Darkness:

Your Word is wrapped in nourishing mystery—now revealed among us as the mass and energy of Christ's love. Help me feel the celebration vibrating at the quantum level of my being, bonding all in the family of living things into your fullness of life itself.

Amen.

■ ■ ■

DECEMBER 4

Christ Jesus, God from God and New Adam:

You are the dark, shimmering light of holiness wrapped in the encompassing form of humanity, in perfect fullness. You mirror back to us what we might be as we participate in what you are.

Amen.

■ ■ ■

DECEMBER 5

Spirit of Advent:

I kneel in the chambered glory of choired harmonies, ready to join in the angel-song to the praise of your past, present, and future coming.

Amen.

■ ■ ■

DECEMBER 6

Gentle Light of Salvation:

Fall upon me with your straight lines directly from the Father by the Spirit, and turn my waiting into praising, that I may reflect to you the goodness of being in the company of the twice born.

Amen.

■ ■ ■

DECEMBER 7

Fierce Light of Prophecy:

I wish to join in the company of John's announcement and see with the eyes of faith the new thing God is doing among the human family so beloved.

From garden to desert, and cross to tomb, your glory encircles this tribe and leaves a trail of faithful ones, kneeling to hear more and obey deeper.

Amen.

■ ■ ■

DECEMBER 8

Tender Light of Creation:

You bless the tenderhearted with a new inclination toward compassion for all things living.

Help me learn the ways of safeguarding the nest of life on planet Earth.

And inspire me to sing songs of praise and gratitude for the gift of being here among the woven universe.

Amen.

DECEMBER 9

Dark Light of Bethlehem:

You open your chasm to shine the stars toward the tender king blooming in the desert.

I wish to listen to the babe's cry in the silence of the dark night and hear humanity's first encounter with the divine majesty touching our earthly estate with royal blood.

Amen.

■ ■ ■

DECEMBER 10

Shimmering Light of Humility:

Never can I stand with the certainty of knowledge other than as an adopted heir of the wisdom from above that guides all through the gospel of consent to the One who released all glory to suffer the defeat of mockery, shame, and death. Let no other shimmering light lead me forward other than the golden light of the Son's self-giving.

Amen.

DECEMBER 11

Starry Advent Light:

With the wise men of the East, light my journey and desire toward Christ's truth and quicken my path of upright action in a contorted culture seeking to make itself grander in its own image rather than being formed in the likeness of your Son.

Amen.

■ ■ ■

DECEMBER 12

Elemental Light of Heaven's Rejoicing:

A darkly radiant vision arises this mid-Advent day.

I see dimly the promises. I feel the cold edge of Herod nearing. I hear the whispers of doubt.

I read the contortions of mythology.

Let me see through the veil of history and feel the upsurge of your glory claiming for itself a holy people of prayer and devotion, joy and praise.

Amen.

DECEMBER 13

Gift Giver for Those Who Ask:

For Christmas, I ask for the gift that you cover my thinking with a canopy of evergreen grace.

Let my mind dwell in the space before light, where silence births all seeing, and stillness calls for every voice of praise.

Amen.

■ ■ ■

DECEMBER 14

Voice within the Silent Scriptures:

Hearing the quiet voice of Advent's prophets, I realize that unheeded wisdom leads to an unbalanced life.

Help me heed your invitation to enter the inner conversation of abiding wonder to join your Word in becoming Adam's lost destiny and Eve's forgotten glory.

Amen.

■ ■ ■

DECEMBER 15

Eternal Word of God:

I pray for the miracle of an imagination not bound by the past, but open to receive a humble, listening heart, inclined toward your Word not yet spoken, but soon to be revealed.

Amen.

■ ■ ■

DECEMBER 16

Firstborn of Mary, Queen of Your Heart:

It is a very human lot to realize too late that one has missed the moment; that a new destiny passed by without notice.

Teach me the openness of Mary, whose body felt the gates of time open, and your Word seeded something new for all of us, all because of her consent.

Teach me the language and logic of her magnificent prayer of consent—*let it be in me*. More than anything, let this course be my Christmas aim.

Amen.

DECEMBER 17

Wholeness of All:

By the wind through the burnt-red leaves, I begin this mid-December Advent day with praise in my heart.

By the far-ranging hills, layered in the blue-gray morning distance, your quiet greets my body, and I begin this day in remembrance, joy, and peace.

Amen.

■ ■ ■

DECEMBER 18

Eternal Strength for My Arising:

A mid-December storm shakes the still morning with house-rattling thunder. Shockingly close lightning rips the sky in two.

The close of Advent draws near.

Prophets boom their voices.

Angels brightly appear.

All around, a sleeping people awakens.

The safe life we so blithely receive each day is overturned in a sacred fraction of your presence's arrival.

Amen.

▓ ▓ ▓

DECEMBER 19

Spirit of the Angels:

Cold air brought freezing morning temperatures, alerting of the nearing solstice, and the lengthening dark nights.

For every shelter and home, we give thanks.

For places to cook hearty meals and take rest, we praise Thee.

May family life be joyful and may gathering be peaceful.

Amen.

▓ ▓ ▓

DECEMBER 20

God in Whom I Abide:

Layered clouds stretch like wavy slate across the morning sky.

Nearly at winter's solstice, the day begins wet and cold.

We sit warm and dry by the fireplace.

May all beings find your love a home, no matter what kind of house or self they dwell in.

We all dwell in you and you in us.

Amen.

■ ■ ■

DECEMBER 21

God of Light:

The unseeing way greets this day. A solstice morning wrapped in deep fog. Last night the full December moon rose, large and red-orange, north on the horizon, then hid in a shroud of cloud.

O God, you are blazing light and heat. Give me faith to follow you even when I can't see or even know you any more than I see and know last night's lost full moon.

Amen.

■ ■ ■

DECEMBER 22

Christ, My Center:

The miracle of Christmas is the reminder that the dignity of being human is our capacity to reflect the whole, as specific parts.

I reflect the light, and thus the light can be seen.

I reflect the gift of Being, and thus Being and its Source can be received a bit more.

Amen.

■ ■ ■

DECEMBER 23

God of All Being, Light in All Darkness:

Remind me when I forget.

Awaken me when I fall asleep.

Raise me when I fall.

So I might fulfill my role and destiny as a mirror of Your Reality—a reflection of Your life and love.

We are each a counterpart to Your infinite light.

Amen.

■ ■ ■

DECEMBER 24

River of Salvation Flowing Forth from Eden:

The deep roots of the Tree of Life reach my ground of being this day.

May the living water of life kiss the growing tips of those ancient roots and unfurl into my being this Christmas the ever-growing Christ in me.

Amen.

DECEMBER 25

O Thou, Lord Jesus, God's Christ, and Spirit's Proceeding:

You are the long-sought answer.

The deeply drawn breath inhaled.

You are the hidden gift, appointed and chosen before time ever came to be.

Amen.

■ ■ ■

DECEMBER 26

Lord Jesus Christ, Sent One:

In the stillness of this winter day, I place my heart upon the silence and hear, as if a witness, speaking of hidden things, of the good wine, served last to me, one late to your table and hearth. I hear you voice forth a word sheared from the depth of your Word's counsels—

Even unseen, and from a vast distance, my countenance is upon you. My ascension still shapes all your heavenward gazing. I came downward as you, with you, and departed upward for you. Let joy guide your

journey, and listen for the counsel of the ancient angels,
guardians of the Christmas treasure until the kingdom
of the dawn light is complete.

Amen.

■ ■ ■

DECEMBER 27

Anointed One for Our Salvation:

In the shadow of Christmas, I lean toward the manger
again, now alone, after the tumult of celebration and family
gatherings.

Seeing through the symbols, my inner mind asks to
understand once again with the angels what has been
accomplished in time for beyond time. As I listen, I receive
the awareness that deep is the way of adoration and strong
is the way of sacrifice. I wish to embody these ways, not just
theologically but also relationally.

Amen.

■ ■ ■

DECEMBER 28

Jesus, Servant to Humankind:

Each day is a gift. I don't begin the day thinking it is my last. I mostly take life for granted, as if the next moment is given. Yet it is not. Each moment, I am being lived, I am being breathed, I am being given the gift of existence. I wish to cherish each day by loving more deeply, caring more thoroughly, attending to others more consistently, and serving more joyfully. May it be so.

Amen.

■ ■ ■

DECEMBER 29

Hearkening Heart of God:

I feel the draw of your love, affecting my every thought with such beneficial joy.

I am yours, Lord. There is no constriction in my volition toward your grace and generosity.

I walk into your broad assistance and find myself buoyed with an inexplicable joy—the joy of my salvation; the joy of giving everything away; the joy of being nobody; the joy of saying yes to your ancient invitation: *yes, I will follow.*

Amen.

■ ■ ■

DECEMBER 30

Creator God of the Heavens and the Earth:

Under the ancient earth and the heavy seas, there is a light flash embedded into all first things. That light is carried by the earth, like a camel through the desert of our universe. Vast open space is filled and overflowing with nothing but itself. And yet here, on this orbed miracle, there is a treasury of glory, a holy temple imprinted with the distilled light that forms words. And most of all the words that birth one Word: *I am with you now and always; I will never leave you or forsake you. Come to me, all who are weary, and I will journey with you and take you and all your ancient burdens into the ease of simply being my beloved.*

Amen.

■ ■ ■

DECEMBER 31

God of Endings, Rendings, and Sendings:

As I reflect upon the year that now completes, through it all I feel that something was purged from my being: regrets of the past and fears of the future.

I stand between an ending and a beginning. My life is a holy remembering, a sacred privilege to dwell at peace in the house of memory.

Help me give an honest and complete accounting. And celebrate who I have been and rejoice in wonder in the possibilities of who I yet may become.

Amen.

A PARTING PRAYER

God of our Journeys:

Your ways with us are so patient and merciful.

You draw light from darkness,

honey from rocks,

water from desert,

manna from night dew,

fire from ash,

peace from violence,

and life from tomb.

Draw us each deeper, as we begin a new year's journey, into the sweetness of love and the light of wisdom.

May the weary ashes of our lifetime be lit once again by the fire of your presence.

Amen.

About Paraclete Press

Paraclete Press is the publishing arm of the Cape Cod Benedictine community, the Community of Jesus. Presenting a full expression of Christian belief and practice, we reflect the ecumenical charism of the Community and its dedication to sacred music, the fine arts, and the written word.

SCAN
TO
READ
MORE

www.paracletepress.com

You may also be interested in...

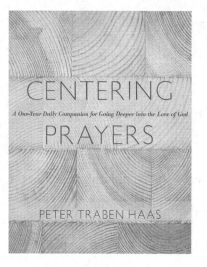

CENTERING

A One-Year Daily Companion for Going Deeper into the Love of God

PRAYERS

PETER TRABEN HAAS

A Daily Devotional for Drawing
Closer to the Heart of God

Centering
Prayers *for*
Women

PETER TRABEN HAAS
FOREWORD BY JUDITH VALENTE